PRAISE FOR THE FIRST EDITION

"Dr. Rona Leach McLeod has provided K–6 teachers with a set of practical applications for developing a culturally responsive classroom. The new edition adds additional strategies and tools that help teachers align their standards and assessments for increased effectiveness in planning for student needs. This book is well organized and simply arranged to address specific needs and issues related to many facets of diversity. The variety of activities that are provided in this book will be a wonderful addition to any teacher's professional library. It is timeless in its approach and lends itself easily to an integrative approach to teaching and learning."—Teresa Reynolds, chair of the Teacher Education Department and Disability Services Program coordinator, St. Andrews University—A Branch of Webber International University, Laurinburg, NC

"Dr. McLeod's book on diversity awareness is clear, to the point, and has universal appeal. Not only are teaching activities provided, but she empowers the reader to look at diversity broadly and from a different perspective—an interesting and innovative approach. I encourage all educators to read this publication."—Garland E. Pierce, North Carolina state representative, District 48, Hoke, Robeson, Richmond, and Scotland counties

"This is a very well-organized and easy-to-follow book for engaging all of our ever-changing diverse student population. Students of all abilities and backgrounds can connect to the wide range of activities and lessons in this book. Dr. McLeod has provided a great resource for teachers to teach diversity and inclusion with focus on all content areas."—Mohsen Ghaffari, fifth grade teacher, and Utah Teacher of the Year (2015), North Star Elementary School, Salt Lake City School District

"Wow! What a great focus and impactful suggestions given throughout this masterpiece as it relates to suggested activities. There are also opportunities for personal reflections and expansion of one's own activities. Excellent opportunity to jumpstart and assist educators with developing and enhancing meaningful activities that will impact student learning and growth."—Rick Singletary, principal, Bennettsville Intermediate School, Marlboro County, South Carolina

"Rona Leach McLeod's book is an excellent resource for teachers looking for material to make the teaching of diversity issues come alive in the classroom. The text can be used in both college and high school classrooms. The tools and exercises provided in this text will serve as an excellent source of material for engaging students in the study of diversity in the school and in the larger community beyond the school."—Robert Hopkins, dean and vice president of academic affairs, St. Andrews University—A Branch of Webber International University, Laurinburg, North Carolina

"Dr. McLeod has again 'hit the mark.' The down-to-earth and user-friendly activities serve as excellent educational resources for teachers to teach as well as to integrate diversity awareness and multicultural education into content. An understanding and awareness of diversity is very much needed to help students as they face the many challenges of our ever-changing world."—Virgie M. Binford, adjunct professor, J. Sargeant Reynolds Community College

"*Diversity Awareness for K–6 Teachers: An Approach to Learning and Understanding Our World* considers diversity from a very broad perspective. The activities in this book encourage students to appreciate the diversity that is all around us. The lessons help students recognize that differences are a natural and wonderful part of our lives. The teaching strategies themselves capitalize on the diversity of learning styles that exist among our students. This is a great resource for all teachers."—Patreese Ingram, assistant dean for multicultural affairs and professor, College of Agricultural Sciences, Pennsylvania State University

Diversity Awareness for K–6 Teachers

Diversity Awareness for K–6 Teachers

An Approach to Learning and Understanding Our World

Second Edition

Rona Leach McLeod

ROWMAN & LITTLEFIELD
Lanham • Boulder • New York • London

Published by Rowman & Littlefield
A wholly owned subsidiary of The Rowman & Littlefield Publishing Group, Inc.
4501 Forbes Boulevard, Suite 200, Lanham, Maryland 20706
www.rowman.com

Unit A, Whitacre Mews, 26-34 Stannary Street, London SE11 4AB

Copyright © 2017 by Rona Leach McLeod

All rights reserved. No part of this book may be reproduced in any form or by any electronic or mechanical means, including information storage and retrieval systems, without written permission from the publisher, except by a reviewer who may quote passages in a review.

British Library Cataloguing in Publication Information Available

Library of Congress Cataloging-in-Publication Data

Names: McLeod, Rona Leach, 1951– author.
Title: Diversity awareness for K–6 teachers : an approach to learning and understanding our world / Rona Leach McLeod.
Description: Second Edition. | Lanham : ROWMAN & LITTLEFIELD, [2017] | Includes bibliographical references.
Identifiers: LCCN 2016057695 (print) | LCCN 2017002110 (ebook) | ISBN 9781475830415 (cloth : alk. paper) | ISBN 9781475830422 (paper : alk. paper) | ISBN 9781475830439 (electronic)
Subjects: LCSH: Culturally relevant pedagogy. | Multicultural education—Activity programs. | Elementary school teaching.
Classification: LCC LC1099.M35 2017 (print) | LCC LC1099 (ebook) | DDC 370.117—dc23
LC record available at https://lccn.loc.gov/2016057695

Contents

Foreword by Dr. Regina McClinton ... xi

Introduction: To the Teacher ... xiii

Activity One: Days of the Week ... 1

Activity Two: Months of the Year ... 4

Activity Three: The Year ... 7

Activity Four: Words ... 11

Activity Five: Colors ... 15

Activity Six: Money ... 18

Activity Seven: Music ... 21

Activity Eight: Food ... 24

Activity Nine: Race and Ethnicity ... 27

Activity Ten: Hats ... 30

Activity Eleven: Age ... 34

Activity Twelve: Continents ... 37

Activity Thirteen: Pets ... 41

Activity Fourteen: Languages ... 44

Activity Fifteen: State Flowers/State Trees/State Birds	47
Activity Sixteen: Length	51
Activity Seventeen: Tools	54
Activity Eighteen: Insects	57
Activity Nineteen: Alphabet Letters	60
Activity Twenty: Greeting Cards	63
Activity Twenty-One: Holidays	66
Activity Twenty-Two: Sports	69
Activity Twenty-Three: States and Capitals	73
Activity Twenty-Four: Road Signs	76
Activity Twenty-Five: Systems and Organs of the Body	79
Activity Twenty-Six: Weather Conditions	82
Activity Twenty-Seven: Shoes	86
Activity Twenty-Eight: Planets	89
Activity Twenty-Nine: Modes of Transportation	92
Activity Thirty: Rocks	96
Activity Thirty-One: Emotions	99
Activity Thirty-Two: Types of Sentences	102
Activity Thirty-Three: Presidents of the United States	106
Activity Thirty-Four: Multiple Intelligences	110
Activity Thirty-Five: Names	113
Activity Thirty-Six: Stores	116
Activity Thirty-Seven: Addresses	119
Activity Thirty-Eight: Birthdays	122
Activity Thirty-Nine: Numbers	125
Activity Forty: Punctuation	129
Activity Forty-One: Sports Mascots	132
Activity Forty-Two: Newspapers	135

Activity Forty-Three: Musical Instruments	138
Activity Forty-Four: Colleges and Universities	141
Activity Forty-Five: Parts of a Tree	145
Activity Forty-Six: Jobs and Occupations	148
Summary	151
Appendix A: Lesson-Plan Format: Diversity Awareness	153
Appendix B: Curriculum Standards	155
Appendix C: Teacher-Suggested Themes	157
Bibliography and Other Resources	159
About the Author	161

Foreword

EDUCATION TODAY IS TRULY a multicultural experience. Each year, the percentage of K–12 students who are ethnic minorities, multiethnic, or recent immigrants and refugees increases. Yet those who teach continue to be from the majority culture, which, in and of itself, is neither bad nor wrong. But when teachers have no connection to the cultures of their students, and the difficulties and issues their students face, conflicts can arise. While research indicates that this "trend" of teachers and students coming from different backgrounds will continue, teachers currently receive insufficient training and support to work across the cultures in their classrooms.

America's teachers want to be successful in educating their students, and are invested in their students' success. *Diversity Awareness for K–6 Teachers: An Approach to Learning and Understanding Our World* was written to provide support, resources, and information to teachers so they can be successful in the daily cross-cultural interactions that occur in education.

Diversity Awareness for K–6 Teachers is an accessible, hands-on tool, and is adaptable to specific curricular standards and needs. The addition of the *Curriculum Standard Identification* tool does well to support this adaptability. Also, it serves to inform, guide, and challenge teachers as they strive to better themselves and be more effective in the classroom, which is aided by use of the *Reflections* section in each activity.

When teachers are able to understand their students and the students' cultural perspectives, they are able to more effectively engage their students and build relationships, which supports students in self-efficacy, motivation, and performance in the classroom. *Diversity Awareness for K–6 Teachers* provides teacher and curricular support in the beginning grades of a student's education career and is so very vital. The foundation of a child's identity, confidence, and resilience are established during his/her first six years of life, but they are not fully set for years to come.

Teachers play a vital role in the development of a child's identity, and if they can be active participants that serve to positively build children's full sense of self, including valuing one's cultural heritage, then they are preparing students to value themselves and education. These efforts may not only support students' long-term academic success, but also support them to go on to be global citizens, and inspire in them a desire to be lifelong learners.

—Regina S. McClinton, PhD, CDP
Director, Intercultural Training Certificate
Grand Valley State University, Michigan

Introduction
To the Teacher

WELCOME TEACHERS AND preservice teachers to a new and revised resource guide, *Diversity Awareness for K–6 Teachers: An Approach to Learning and Understanding Our World*. As a twenty-first-century teacher, you are held accountable for the achievement level of each of your students. This means valuable teaching resources and tools are a necessity.

One of the most valuable talents and skills of a teacher is the ability to teach content and teach in a way such that every child comprehends and learns. Additionally, as teachers, we want to engage every child in lessons to ensure they learn and enjoy learning. This resource guide has been designed using activities that are engaging and enjoyable for you as the teacher to teach and instruct your students. Many activities are a part of this guide, but space is also provided to create and develop other academic activities across various content areas.

The activities can be used as shared within this guide, or they can be modified by you, the teacher, to meet the needs of your students. You have the opportunity to develop and record additional themes in the back of this book. It is designed to be ever-changing, relevant, and user-friendly. This guide will also serve as an excellent source of documentation on standards taught, and the success level of each standard.

States have adopted standards-based curricula. Review the specific standards for your grade level and content area in order to use this guide to the fullest. *Diversity Awareness for K–6 Teachers: An Approach to Learning and Understanding Our World* has been designed, not in isolation of a standards-based curriculum, but to serve as an additional tool to ensure standards are taught and pertinent instructional information is documented.

A sample lesson-plan format has been included as an appendix to this guide for your use. Feel free to modify this to meet your particular needs. Lastly, add to this guide other relevant themes and activities. As you read through the guide, other themes/topics will come to mind and may be useful to integrate into your specific content areas. I hope that this guide will help you to continue to learn and grow as a dynamic and effective teacher!

PERSONAL REFLECTION

Reflecting on How I Learn

The topic of diversity is open to very broad interpretation. One assumption, however, when speaking of "diversity," is that it means something set apart, or something different. One of the best places to begin understanding diversity is to conduct a candid self-assessment of how you, as the teacher, learn. Once you reflect on and understand how you best learn, you can then become more tolerant of the learning style preferences of students within your classroom. Please take a closer look at yourself before using these activities/themes, and determine how your learning may impact the way you instruct your students.

Assume the role of "student," and take a few minutes to work on each activity. Be candid about your responses and reflections. As you begin to engage in the various activities, your perception may change somewhat. You will find yourself being able to develop multiple classroom diversity–related activities while integrating diversity into your curriculum standards. Again, assess by self-administering each activity to determine how you will respond. Feel free to modify themes and activities to address your classroom needs.

Reflecting on How My Students Learn

Knowing each of your students is of paramount importance. How does that student learn? As you reflect on your own learning preference, you will become more mindful of the learning preferences of your students. This in itself is diversity. We just learn differently!

You will become more aware of your strengths and weaknesses as well as the strengths and weaknesses of your students. Critically assessing the learning styles, strengths, and weaknesses of your students will enable you, as the teacher, to be more successful and effective in taking each student from where he/she is, to his/her highest achieving potential.

Research

Research on how children learn is ever-changing. What we knew about how we learned a decade ago is not the same as what we know today. Keep up with the latest learning and brain research. Teachers are "action researchers." We are constantly asking questions, solving problems, and looking for more effective ways to teach. Knowledge seeking and continuous learning are key to ensuring that our students learn.

The themes and activities presented in this guide are fun, energizing, and serve as another resource for teaching and learning. Continue to generate and record new themes and activities to promote learning. Have fun, teach, learn, and enjoy!

Activity One

Days of the Week

LET'S START OFF WITH A theme activity that is relevant for every student in your class. This activity allows every student to participate and share his/her experiences as they relate to the days of the week. This activity has been designed to spark excitement with a high level of sharing and comparing.

Exploring the days of the week is a delightful, fun-filled way to motivate and get students actively involved in discussion, input, and even interesting suggestions. As the teacher, please share your own experiences regarding the days of the week with your students. Everyone has an opinion about this activity. Allow your students time to discuss how the days are alike and how they differ. This is a wonderful way to begin an introduction to diversity, showing how the days differ and the importance of each day to everyone.

OUTLINED SUGGESTED ACTIVITIES

NOTE: Themes/Activities can be used across various content areas.

1. Language Arts: Under Activity Three, read the poem *Different Days Make the Year*, and ask students to compare and contrast the differences you can experience in a week. How do these days contribute to make a week, and a year, in a person's life?
2. Have students discuss differences in the daily roles of the children and adults in their household. How do differences in the roles help the family operate successfully? How and why are these differences important? How does everyone contributing their fair share help the whole family?

3. Have students talk about differences in human beings. Facilitate this discussion very closely. Do these differences contribute to the betterment of our community, state, nation, and our world? Do all people have something positive to offer? How do differences in the days of the week compare to differences in human beings? Is there a comparison? List the different explanations. Have students explain how they arrived at their answers.
4. Talk about the school environment. Do all students and adults have the same roles and daily responsibilities? Does each role/responsibility contribute to the success of the school and classroom? How will the outcome of the roles and responsibilities of members of the school environment impact the success of the school day?
5. Art and Science: Teacher and students can also post pictorial representations of what happens during the five days of the school week. They can discuss the weather outcome for each day, and also discuss what fun they had each day of the week, even though the days may have been different. Different days still have gifts to offer. What were some of the positives and negatives of each day?
6. History and Technology: Establish "day teams" in your class. Have each team use the Internet to conduct a special study of their assigned day of the week. Students can later discuss and share their research findings.
7. Be creative and think of other activities your students may be able to conduct with the days of the week activity.

Final thought for Activity One: If every day is the same, we would not be able to experience nor share the many gifts that each unique day brings to our lives.

- This activity can open up conversation and allow for the creativity to integrate this lesson with other lessons.
- Another good idea is to have your students *draw* their favorite day of the week. How can they represent this day in picture form? What makes this day cool? Post the results in the classroom. This may make for some interesting drawings and interpretations. The diversity of thought put into this assignment by students can be extraordinary. How are the drawings of students who chose the same favorite day different and/or alike?
- Assign students to small groups. Have them develop an original song or rap about the days of the week or their favorite day. Make sure you set ground rules for this assignment.
- Class activity: Create a play about the days of the week. If possible, involve parents in helping to design days of the week costumes. Present the play at a PTA meeting or a Parents' Night event.
- With your students, prepare a day of the week bulletin board.
- You have only scratched the surface of a world of ideas for activities that will enhance your students' creativity, problem solving, and critical thinking skills.

Refer to Appendix B to record your own curriculum standards.

OTHER TEACHER-SUGGESTED ACTIVITIES

Activity Two

Months of the Year

JUST AS FOR THE days of the week, delightful instructional activities and learning experiences can be generated for the months of the year. Create a classroom atmosphere where your focus starts on the present month. Consider the age of your students to determine your approach. If students are young, they may or may not know the twelve months of the year. What experiences do they bring to your classroom? What are their birth months? Start with their areas of familiarity. If they can relate, they will get involved. Can they categorize months in any manner? Is a suggested month a warm or cold month? What types of clothing might be worn during certain months?

Take one month at a time and teach across the curriculum. See the vast opportunities for teaching and learning about our world you now have at your fingertips. Explore the monthly diversity of holidays, presidential recognitions, civic leaders, and special days in specific months, such as Valentine's Day, Mother's Day, Earth Day, Veterans Day, and so on. The list of teachable moments goes on.

OUTLINED SUGGESTED ACTIVITIES

1. Science and Social Studies: Have students research their birth month. Suggestions include:
   - Select ten characteristics of the birth month.
   - List five famous people who were born during the selected month, and share their contributions. This will give students the opportunity to conduct structured research.

- What types of flowers or plants are commonly found in your region during the student's birth month?

2. Science: Document and discuss, as a class, the weather characteristics for each of the twelve months. Describe these on a table in the classroom for easy viewing on a display board. Research and discuss general weather conditions during the months of the year.
3. Divide students into groups to study the twelve months of the year. Each group will be responsible for developing a collage of occurrences during their assigned month.
4. Talk about "What if we missed a month?" What are some possibilities if this would happen? Why do we need the diversity of the months of the year?
5. Hold student debates. What is the most important month of the year, and why?
6. What are some commonly available vegetables and fruits in your part of the country during specific months?
7. Language Arts and Drama: Assist students in developing a short skit on "The Missing Month!" How would this change our world?
8. Language Arts: Write short stories and plays.
9. List holidays that are a part of each month. Study the history behind each of these holidays.
10. Social Studies: Have students study significant events that have occurred in history during each of the twelve months.
11. Music: Create a special holiday song for each month. Get everyone involved!
12. This is a great opportunity to encourage students from different states and countries to share a part of their culture and history. What special songs are sung during special holidays in different states and countries?
13. Encourage your students' creativity. Have them develop their own month of the year. How would it look? This really inspires diversity in thought and response. Discuss some of the major characteristics of this newly developed month. Might it combine characteristics from the other months?

Refer to Appendix B to record your own curriculum standards.

OTHER TEACHER-SUGGESTED ACTIVITIES

Activity Three

The Year

THIS IS A WONDERFUL OPPORTUNITY to create lessons with emphasis on "comparing and contrasting." A strong starting point is teacher-developed activities applicable to the present year. The current year provides dynamic opportunities to teach social studies and history, as well as other content areas. What primary world events occurred on this day last year, in comparison to the current day and year? Build a solid base, first on "the present," and then venture out by researching, studying, comparing, contrasting, and even developing a process of predicting possibilities for the future. Think outside the box as to what activities you can develop to tie in with the present year, past years, and even the future.

OUTLINED SUGGESTED ACTIVITIES

1. Just as with the months of the year, have your students research their birth year. Develop a chart that includes the years in which students were born. Recognize that there may be little diversity for this activity because most students were born within the same year. See how this activity develops as you move into other suggested activities. Research famous people who may have been born in a particular year. You may even select specific categories of people such as: scientists, inventors, teachers, business owners, and so on.
2. Select specific years for students to research. Have them work in cooperative groups of three to four students. This can be an individual, group, or whole class activity, which in itself demonstrates how students can work and learn in diverse classroom learning groups.

3. Social Studies and History: What important things happened during particular years, and how have these events impacted our world today?
4. Language Arts: Have students write essays such as: What if we did not have the year 1968 or 1950 (or any other year of your choice) carved in our history?
5. Discuss with students the best year of their lives. Was it when they got their first bike? What made that year so special? Was there a year that brought sadness? Did a student lose a pet? You, as the teacher, can also take part in this activity.
6. Science: Have students conduct scientific research about hurricanes and other significant weather conditions occurring each year, or use a five-year cycle of study.
7. Creative Activity: If you could design a perfect year, how would it look, and why?
8. Art: Have students draw their favorite year in the form of a picture and explain its meaning. Post these drawings in the classroom for future reference. At the end of the year, have them draw another picture to depict their year of learning. Redesign this activity in any way you wish. Students can compare and contrast, and explore the diversity of events of various years.

These activities will give students a sense that years are indeed different in terms of the experiences we share, some positive and others negative. This leads to a lot of diversity in life.

Refer to Appendix B to record your own curriculum standards.

Different Days Make the Year

Each day wears a different outfit
Of a dress, a suit, or perhaps a tie.
It brings to us a special and wonderful gift
We can receive if we only try.

Just think of a bright, warm and sunny day
Wearing a swimsuit and a tan,
It brings fun, laughter and swimming too
And we can even play in the backyard sand.

Another day may be a cloudy day,
Dressed in a cap, shoes, and sweater
Protecting us from the sun's warm rays
Will make this day even better.

The Year

Just think of a cold wintry day,
Wrapped in boots, gloves, coat and hat.
You can see your breath as you exhale
Wondering when you will be called in is your bet.

Oh, not today it's raining outside
Which calls for a raincoat and galoshes
If I can just jump in that big old puddle
And make it back to the dryer and washer!

July is a long time from a snowy day
When I can build a snowman and have snow fights
But I must be patient and wait for the time
Which gives the world a beautiful and welcome sight.

Each day is different but it makes "a year"
Sporting a special outfit of its own kind
Whether dressed in a raincoat, suit, or blue jeans
Special in giving and happiness for you to find.

Just as the days, we too are different
How boring if we were all the same
But all of our differences paint a picture
Captured within a lovely picture frame.

Other Teacher-Suggested Activities

Activity Four

Words

WORDS ARE SO MUCH A part of our existence. Think about a day without this form of oral and written communication. There are endless ways you can approach teaching across the curriculum using words and creating an awareness of differences and similarities. Think about ways you can show the power of words in our society.

This activity is designed to allow students to become actively engaged and creative with poetry, prose, art, and rap. The teacher is the driving force behind this activity in leading discussions about tolerance and the need to respect others within and outside of the classroom setting. Quite often diversity can lead to name calling. A strong discussion about respecting each other's differences is very important to lead into this activity. Adjust activities to the appropriate grade level and to serve the needs of your students. The following is an introduction to a rich selection of activities, discussion, and creativity.

Words CAN

Bring smiles to your face
Bring tears to your eyes
Make you feel welcome
Make you feel unwelcome
Make you glad
Make you feel sad
Make the load lighter
Make the day brighter

Make you feel good on the inside
Make you feel bad on the inside
Embarrass you
Comfort you
Lift your spirit
Bring you down

Words CANNOT determine who you are in life.

OUTLINED SUGGESTED ACTIVITIES

1. Start the activity by reading the poem, then move into a discussion. You might also want to research and find a children's book that would be a good lead-in to this activity.
2. Read the above "Words CAN" and "Words CANNOT" statements to students, and have them react to each one. This will probably generate lots of discussion and excitement among students.
3. Art: Have students draw pictures of each statement. Several students might draw pictures of their interpretations. Have each student discuss the meaning behind their drawing. This represents diversity in terms of how each student perceives the statement. Become actively involved in the activities, so that students can hear your reactions.
4. Have a "Be Kind to Others Day." Instruct students to say something truthful, but kind, to another student in their classroom. It could be just speaking to someone, or letting them know that his/her hair looks pretty. At day's end, provide a time for students to share with you and the class how they felt about the positive words.
5. Work toward incorporating a Be Kind To Others Day throughout the school. Get students to answer how they would organize this day and what they could do to share the idea of speaking kind words instead of hurtful words to students throughout the school.
6. Pair students who may not normally work together. Have each pair design a personal list of "Words CAN" and "Words CANNOT" as poetry, prose, or rap. Post their creations in the classroom. Each thought may be different, but each is an expression of how they feel and the impact words have had on their young lives.
7. Reading: Use the children's story "Cinderella" to illustrate to students how words had an impact on her life. Can students pick out words in the story that made Cinderella feel sad, happy, embarrassed, down, confused, and so on? Select other stories that have good illustrations.

8. Language Arts: Select ten to twelve words that make up a sentence, and duplicate the words for several groups in your class. Have students work in groups to create one or more sentences using these words. Each group will have the same words, but may develop a completely different sentence. Gear this activity to the age level of your students. You may also allow each group to add several words of their choice to the assigned words.
9. As you become involved in the above activities, they will generate other wonderful and exciting ideas for even stronger student activities for learning and gaining a better understanding of our world.

Refer to Appendix B to record your own curriculum standards.

Other Teacher-Suggested Activities

Activity Five

Colors

GET READY FOR A lively classroom environment! Colors will afford you the opportunity to be creative with a number of activities addressing diversity and tolerance. Engage in art and science activities with students as they create various colors using paints and crayons. How many different colors can students create? Ask questions such as: If everything in the classroom was represented by the same color, what would you see? Engage students in critical thinking. The following suggestions will allow you to expand into and integrate different subjects within the classroom setting.

OUTLINED SUGGESTED ACTIVITIES

1. Mathematics and Graphing: Have students select a favorite color. Some will select the same color, and that is perfectly okay. Work with students on an activity to graph the colors of their choice on a bar graph (for example, seven red, eight blue, three purple, two green, and so on). With the colors selected, percentages of each color can be determined if you are working with upper-level elementary students. After graphing has been completed, narrow the selection down to three or four of the top choices. You might also be creative and use a similar activity using jelly beans. You have now eliminated several of the colors as a result of the jelly beans! Jelly beans just may disappear.
2. Science: Think of eliminating colors from the environment. For example, if green was eliminated, discuss how the earth's environment and plant world would be impacted. Green in plants represents chlorophyll. How might this

impact our world? Weave this discussion into diversity. How might the lack of green impact plant and animal life?

3. Continue with discussing eliminating other colors, stressing how the world might be if we were without those colors in nature. Have students come up with hypothesis statements. This will help to impress on students that all colors are not the same, but each is very important. Lots of discussion and some interesting ideas may come from this activity. Students may generate other activity ideas.

4. Language Arts: Put students in groups of three. Have them develop a story, "The Missing Color!" Give each group a limit of several pages for their story and several days of class activity time to get together and develop their unique stories. Each story will have the same theme, but a different beginning, middle, and end. This will give students an opportunity to be creative, work together in groups, share diverse ideas, and come together to develop a work of art. Be creative in how you would like the activity to progress.

5. Art: Assign a special project for your art class. Students love to draw and be creative. As one requirement, allow them to use only selected colors. After they have completed their activity, have them react to how they felt about using only the selected colors. They may also do the same activity using all the colors. How do the pictures differ? How do students now feel about their last drawing compared to the first?

6. Music: Work with students on a color song!

7. Select a day of the week to wear special colors. Discuss certain holidays or special days represented by certain colors. What is the significance of a particular color?

8. Work with students on the primary colors. Show them how other colors are derived from primary colors. Have students locate these colors within the classroom setting, within the building, and within the school environment.

Refer to Appendix B to record your own curriculum standards.

Other Teacher-Suggested Activities

Activity Six

Money

ALL OF YOUR STUDENTS WILL HAVE some type of experience with money. The experiences will vary, but the students will come to you with some frame of reference about money, its value, and its importance. Start off by assigning students various money values and ask them to share what they would like to do or can do with 1 dollar, 10 dollars, 20 dollars, a quarter, and so on. Share and review different coins and talk about each. What information might you find on a nickel, dime, quarter, and so on? What is the significance of this information?

There are many diversity activities that can be implemented in mathematics, science, and other content areas relating to money. Activities using money will be exciting and high energy. Some students may get weekly allowances, go shopping, or help to purchase items with their families. Students bring money to school and buy school supplies and snacks. They purchase gifts with money. The following are just a few classroom activity ideas that may generate energy, excitement, and lots of learning in your classroom.

OUTLINED SUGGESTED ACTIVITIES

1. Social Studies: Integrate money matters into a lesson. Work with students as they research and compare money from various countries. Compare and contrast.
2. History and Social Studies: Discuss why we need money in our society. Research and discuss various occupations and salaries associated with each. Research the responsibilities of each occupation and required educational backgrounds.

3. History: Research with students the history of money and how it has changed over the years.
4. Mathematics: Develop math lessons to compare different units of money: pennies, dimes, nickels, dollar bills, fives, tens, and so on.
5. Mathematics: Assign groups of students a specific amount of money, such as $153.00 or $233.44. Ask them to achieve the designated total you have assigned them by using various units of money (dollars, dimes, nickels, quarters, pennies, and any units of currency or coins of money of their choice). Are the outcomes the same? Different sets of coins and bills can be used while achieving the same outcome and total. This an excellent illustration of diversity of how we think and process. The objective is for each group to use money to achieve the total of the amount you have requested.
6. Create art lessons where students use different colors of construction paper to cut out different units of money of coins and currency.
7. Establish a store where students can use their classroom money to purchase items. Have students count out money using their selected coins and bills to purchase items. Feel free to use sets of commercial money if you have these available in your classroom. If not, students can of course create their own money from paper.
8. Later on, have several students play the role of the store clerk. Their classmates can come to the student store and purchase items using their desired coins and bills. If a student prefers to pay with one hundred pennies versus four quarters, that is okay. Again, diversity is at work.
9. Have students cut out food items for sale in the newspaper and create money activities around the assignment.
10. Mathematics: Instruct students to select a coin or bill of their choice, or assign students various coins and bills. Provide a wide range of coins, and make sure the selected coins and bills fit with the mathematical problems you assign. Develop a game of "placements" with math problems (addition, subtraction, division, and/or multiplication). Students can become human placements. Assign problems so students can dramatize these problems by placing themselves in proper placement locations. Have students demonstrate one, two, three, or four placements, such as $427.00: for example, 400 + 20 + 7 dollars. An example for younger children: 43 cents = 40 + 3 cents. Again, be creative with this activity.
11. Work with students on a number of problems, then allow them to move around the classroom and create mathematical answers for the dollar amount. They can then see the diversity of money and how each amount is important to the total. These are examples of logical/mathematical and bodily/kinesthetic multiple intelligence activities. Continue to create activities where students can get up and move around.

Refer to Appendix B to record your own curriculum standards.

Other Teacher-Suggested Activities

Activity Seven

Music

Music is universal, and it is important to teach this to our children. There is a rich diversity of music, with many different varieties from all over the world. There are many activities you, as a classroom teacher, can develop to enhance appreciation of this diversity, and to get children actively involved in the lessons. Most children like some form of music. It is your goal to capture their interests while sharing with each child a level of awareness and appreciation for different types and styles of music.

Listen to the music, study the music, dance to the music, and enjoy. Start off with different types of music from the United States and venture out to other countries. Create educational and delightful activities around the various content areas. Study the meaning of music for different ceremonies and activities. Students will gain a deeper understanding and appreciation for different types of music.

OUTLINED SUGGESTED ACTIVITIES

1. Social Studies and Music: Social studies is a great place to begin to integrate and study different types of music. As students study different cultures, make sure to highlight and discuss the history and types of music of each culture.
2. Television and Music: Start off with a discussion of how music is used to drive television programs and hold the attention of the viewers. How does the music sound when a program first comes on the screen? How does music change when someone is in danger? Can music be used in media to alert the viewer of a major surprise? Have students cite examples.

3. Use a popular "educational" video/DVD in your classroom for discussion, and have students analyze the music they hear. What can students determine from the change in the music? Note that different students may have different responses.
4. Ask students to discuss their favorite type of music and why it is their favorite. Remember to have them discuss their favorite *type* of music, not their favorite music personality or group. That can come later.
5. Another way for students to appreciate diversity in music is to generate a discussion about different events and how each can be associated with different music. Examples: baseball games, weddings, and special holidays.
6. Generate a discussion about different types of music, such as country and western, spiritual, hip-hop, jazz, classical, and rock 'n' roll.
7. Pair students to write reports on the history of music. Allow pairs to select their choice of music. Once students understand different types of music, they can gain a better respect and appreciation for the differences.
8. A study of music can also be integrated into a study of different types of musical instruments. Students will find this fascinating. Different instruments produce different sounds, which help to provide music's "uniqueness."
9. Invite visitors to come to your classroom and discuss various instruments, play music, and talk with students about the history of both the music and the instrument.
10. Art: During art and/or social studies classes, have students make and display instruments in the classroom.
11. As the teacher, introduce students to unfamiliar instruments. Study the history and purpose of the instruments. Work with students as they engage in a study of categories of instruments, such as woodwind, percussion, or string instruments. Include in the study the significance of various musical instruments in particular regions of the United States and the world (for example, drums are used for communication in some parts of Africa).
12. You may have students who can play certain instruments; if so, this is a good opportunity to allow them to bring their instruments to class and put on a classroom concert.
13. Over several class periods, allow students to listen to music played on different instruments. Open a discussion with their interpretations of the music. Can students identify musical instruments by listening to the music?
14. If you, the teacher, play an instrument, demonstrate it to your class and conduct a study of your instrument.
15. If possible, attend a special concert with your students. When you return, have an in-depth discussion about the music and different instruments. This would make for a delightful and informative field trip. Invite parents to come along and be a part of this musical extravaganza!

Refer to Appendix B to record your own curriculum standards.

OTHER TEACHER-SUGGESTED ACTIVITIES

Activity Eight

Food

Food is another excellent way to integrate diversity lessons into your curriculum. Everyone has his or her favorite foods. Embrace this opportunity to research together, and study food labels. Why does the body need a variety of foods? Talk about environments that are conducive to growing certain types of food. These activities can enrich the study of health, physical education, science, and social studies.

OUTLINED SUGGESTED ACTIVITIES

1. Health and Science: Students can study various foods and the food groups. Gear your lesson to meet the developmental needs of your students. You can engage your students in a study of the nutritional value of different foods.
2. Have each student write his/her one favorite food on a 3" x 5" card. Post the listings in the classroom and have students get involved in a study of these selections. What are the disadvantages and advantages of each selected food? Are the favorite foods similar, or is there a variety? More than likely, there will be a variety of foods suggested by students. This in itself is diversity. Where do these foods fall within the food groups? Study nutritional values of different types of foods.
3. Health: Conduct a study of the food groups to help students understand the importance of eating healthy and consuming a variety of minerals and vitamins to promote a healthy body.

4. Have students cut out pictures and develop separate collages representing the major food groups. Post in your classroom. Discuss why choosing a variety of foods is healthy.
5. Allow students to bring food labels from home and study the nutritional values indicated on the labels. Mathematics lessons can be developed from the activity for upper-level students. Work with percentages of one ingredient versus another, and so forth. Graph the compositional makeup shown on the labels. A variety of math problems can be derived from such an activity.
6. Music: Have students become creative and design food group songs! It may be a good idea to assign a specific food group to students so they can work together on projects.
7. Continue to study food labels and talk about nutritional values throughout this study.

Refer to Appendix B to record your own curriculum standards.

OTHER TEACHER-SUGGESTED ACTIVITIES

Activity Nine

Race and Ethnicity

CLASSROOMS ARE MORE RACIALLY AND ethnically diverse than ever before. Teaching about racial and ethnic diversity can be rewarding and pave the way toward students respecting each other as human beings. We can look back in time and study the many contributions of people from various racial and ethnic backgrounds. Work with your students as they study contemporary issues and how people from different backgrounds have contributed to solving these issues. You are now opening up an area where we can learn and gain a better understanding of our world.

This activity will allow you, the teacher, to follow up on current racial issues, and will help students achieve a deeper awareness and understanding of racial and ethnic diversity and tolerance. The following activities are only a few examples of what teachers can use and further develop to teach about racial differences.

1. Students can explore newspaper articles to spark a discussion on racial issues, especially relating to school. Have students bring in news articles to read and discuss with the class. This will get them going on special research and fact-finding adventures.
2. Start with a general discussion of race and ethnicity. Outline with students a few of the many racial and ethnic groups, such as African American, Caucasian, Native American, Hispanic, and so on. Give your students an opportunity to discuss racial diversity.
3. Make sure you have representations of diversity on your classroom posters and pictures.

4. Divide students into groups of three and four for special projects. Have them select a racial or ethnic group, perhaps one with which they are not familiar. As part of this assignment, students could report on famous people who represent the group they chose. Encourage them to research people of the past as well as the present.
5. Social Studies: Assign categories such as human relations, music, art, politics, medicine, education, science, and so on. Have them identify people in these categories from the various racial or ethnic groups. For instance, who in the assigned group has contributed greatly to politics?
6. Bring to light people whom students may not know are from different racial groups, and discuss their contributions to the world.
7. Discuss with students how contributions from people of various races or ethnicities benefit all mankind. Have them talk about and bring to the table their favorite personalities of all races, and discuss their contributions to the world. Discuss how the world might be today without the contributions of the many races of people.
8. Social Studies: As students learn about different countries of the world, have them share their knowledge about the many races and ethnic groups representing these countries.
9. Science: A study of inventions may be an interesting topic to research with your students. Share with them various inventions and study the inventors. This will shed light on people of different backgrounds who have invented technology that has made a global impact. Examples include the computer, traffic lights, the automobile, drones, and so on.

Refer to Appendix B to record your own curriculum standards.

OTHER TEACHER-SUGGESTED ACTIVITIES

Activity Ten

―――――◯―――――

Hats

Hats are very much a part of American culture. They are symbolic. We use them in certain ceremonies and activities, as well as to express individuality. Every student in your class more than likely can relate to these activities and bring a wealth of different experiences and conversation to the suggestions. You can conduct similar activities on the topic of shoes.

Talk about categories, and how we can identify people of certain professions by the types of hats they wear: doctors, chefs, religious leaders, and firefighters, just to name a few. This is just one more direction in which you can move to develop strong, fun, and instructional activities.

Introduce your hats activities by presenting them to your students in your own way, leading into a study of diversity. If you are engaged in social studies or geography themes, you might wear a hat representing a particular part of the world or culture. For example, if your class is studying the history and culture of Mexico, you might wear a sombrero. This will give way to a lively classroom discussion. Early on, define what you mean by "a hat" so that everyone is speaking from the same frame of reference.

Outlined Suggested Activities

1. Enhance your opening presentation by setting parameters for categories of hats. List on the board, Smart Board, or chart paper some of the more familiar categories of hats, as well as situations when we most often wear hats. Several examples of categories/situations are listed below:

- Military
- Various professions
- Weather conditions
- School/college graduation
- Religious ceremonies
- Sports
- Holiday celebrations
- Birthdays
- Beach

2. Narrow down your categories/situations as desired. Remember, this is a high-energy discussion because each student may have something different to offer. With a list shared by the students, you can observe the high level of diversity about hats. What a wonderful way to teach about diversity. Even though the hats may be different, each serves a specific purpose, whether the purpose is a celebration, a situation, or a personal preference.
3. Use magazines in the classroom to select pictures of hats. Assist students as they research hats on the Internet. Categorize the hats.
4. Art: Have students design their favorite hat.
5. Establish a "Hat Day" at school or in your classroom. Each student must be able to give the history/background of his or her hat, along with what makes their hat different from other hats and why it is significant. Before giving this assignment, make sure specific guidelines and directions are shared with students, and that the assignment is age appropriate.
6. Have students draw their hats and write a few paragraphs about their favorite hat. Read children's books on hats.
7. Write letters to parents with the assistance of your students. This is a special class project and should involve all of your students. Invite parents and grandparents to come to school with their unique hat and share its meaning and significance. Some participants may wear the hat of a deceased loved one. This may be a way of remembering that person. Think of other variations of Hat Day you might use.
8. Read Across America: Integrate hats activities into Dr. Seuss Day. Study the meaning of the Dr. Seuss hat.
9. Invite people who work in different professions to Hat Day. Do they wear special hats? Examples: police officer, firefighter, pilot, cook, construction worker, surgeon, and so on. Students will develop an even greater appreciation, awareness, and respect for diversity that has been expressed through hats.
10. Art: Make hats that are symbolic of major holidays and special events in the lives of your students. Study hats from different cultures.
11. You might establish in your classroom or school a Celebration of Diversity Day by using hats. Get other community people involved. Invite parents

from various ethnic groups to come and participate in a parade of hats. Men, women, boys, and girls can model their favorite hat. Assign a student or parent to read the history or significance of each hat to the class, so all can enhance their awareness and learning about our world.
12. Music: Modify classroom activities as deemed appropriate. Select several students to create a hat song for this celebration. Read books about hats, such as *The Cat in the Hat*.

Refer to Appendix B to record your own curriculum standards.

OTHER TEACHER-SUGGESTED ACTIVITIES

Activity Eleven

―――――○―――――

Age

THERE IS MUCH DIVERSITY TO BE taught on the subject of age, especially in regard to age level and age-appropriate activities. For example, characteristics of children up to the age of five are not normally shared by children ages six to ten, and so on. Now is your opportunity to utilize this common factor of age to teach diversity and its importance.

OUTLINED SUGGESTED ACTIVITIES

1. Generate a conversation within your class about your students' favorite daily activities. Have students talk about some of their favorite fun activities. How are they different and how are they alike? Have students discuss what might be the favorite daily activities of their parents, and of their grandparents. Are these activities different? If so, why would one group prefer one type of activity, while another would prefer other activities?
2. Divide ages into spans for your class, such as under age five, ages six through twelve, teenagers, young adults, middle-aged adults, and senior citizens. Students can use the age spans you assign them to discuss diversity as it relates to the ages of groups of people.
3. Character Education: Integrate character education activities into your discussion, such as responsibility. Discuss the various levels of responsibility that the following activities might entail as a result of age of the child. Use your designated age levels if the above are not appropriate. Feel free to outline your suggested activities. Lastly, have students share life activities, assign the appropriate age level, and discuss responsibility at that level. Examples:

- Crying when hungry
- Completing fourth-grade homework
- Driving a car alone for the first time
- Pulling objects off the table
- Walking with a cane
- Cooking a full-course meal

What are some of the responsibilities of a sixteen-year-old athlete playing in a baseball game in which her team is losing? What are some of the responsibilities of a thirty-eight-year-old father with three children and a wife? What are some of the responsibilities of a student who is in first grade? Compile your question preferences.

4. Physical Education: Develop a short list of physical fitness activities. Assign age-level clusters and have students pair activities with the age-appropriate groupings outlined in number 2 of this list. Make sure to stress that sometimes age-appropriate activities may not apply. For example, a senior citizen of age seventy may be able to accomplish tasks that younger people cannot.
5. Below is a sample of activities for which students can assign age levels. Feel free to design your list.

- Riding a tricycle
- Skipping rope
- Swimming
- Playing tennis
- Baking a cake
- Jumping rope
- Climbing a tree
- Taking a slow walk
- Gardening
- Playing football/basketball

After the above activity has been comfortably completed by students, have them select their personal physical activities and assign to each an age-appropriate level. Remember, some activities may be appropriate for more than one age level. Share with your students the ages of people who, from childhood to adulthood, have contributed immensely to the world as a whole. Integrate history and the contributions of King Tut and others to the world. Students will be able to see that every person, in his/her own way, can make a positive difference in the lives of other human beings.
6. Engage students in a fact-finding tour to determine the youngest person to accomplish certain tasks. Outline specific tasks for students to study.

Refer to Appendix B to record your own curriculum standards.

Other Teacher-Suggested Activities

Activity Twelve

---○---

Continents

THE STUDY OF THE CONTINENTS presents dynamic opportunities to learn more about different places and people of the world. Have students learn about the location and size of the continents, land masses and physical features, climatic conditions, cultures, primary languages, history, and religions of the people in various countries on the continents. Engage in studies of the animal and plant life indigenous to specific continents.

There is so much you can teach about the similarities and differences of the seven continents. Use special resources such as virtual field trips, the Discovery Channel, and public broadcasting education channels to add strong visuals to the continental study. Help your students discover the richness and beauty of such a wide range of diversity.

The following activities are geared toward upper-level elementary grades. If used for lower-level grades, adjust for the age-appropriate level and curricular content study for students. Have fun while learning and understanding our world!

OUTLINED SUGGESTED ACTIVITIES

1. Social Studies/Technology: As you engage in lessons devoted to various countries of the world, explore the larger bodies of land. Introduce students to the many landforms of the various continents. Make sure they get a real sense of the vastness of these landforms. Virtual field trips will allow students to feel as though they are there!

2. Geography/Technology: Integrate map, globe, and Internet studies into your lessons. These areas are very exciting and will be an interactive means of teaching and learning with your students. This study will provide opportunities to engage in numerous global-awareness activities for students. Utilize the "speaking globe" to help students learn about continents and also various countries. Seek out appropriate games for students to explore the continents. Students can work with the globe independently while checking their responses.
3. If possible, share VHS and DVD presentations on continents or a specific continent. If you have a student or students from another country, have them share about their country and continent with classmates. Watch National Geographic presentations on continents, and discuss as a class.
4. Set up classroom displays about the continents. Make the setup visual and hands-on, so students can quickly identify continents based on shape, size, location, topography, and other characteristics.
5. Explore in-depth specifics about continents, such as languages, primary landforms, racial diversity, foods, music, government, and other areas of interest. This again allows you, as the teacher, to explore all types of diversity issues.
6. Give students opportunities to work as a class as well as in smaller cooperative groups on projects related to the continents.
7. With the massive amount of information available, you may integrate a number of continental study activities over several weeks. If there are newsworthy issues occurring on a specific continent, use the media to study and share with your students.
8. Music, Art, and Dance: Work with your students in the arts where you discuss, share, and listen to the music, and observe the dance and art of each continent. Students can compare and contrast various issues. What are some similarities? What are some differences? People from different countries may have different traditions; therefore, your class is focusing on the overall representation of a continent.
9. Technology: After concluding activities for this topic, have students work together (in groups of four) to prepare and develop a PowerPoint presentation on the continent of their choice, or assign each group a specific continent. Assign information you would like each group to include as a part of the presentation. There are numerous other activity ideas you might generate for this study of the continents.
10. Collaborate with local colleges/universities. If there are students or professors from other continents, invite them to come to your class and share a presentation with your students.

11. Collaborate with people in your community. Quite often there are community members who have visited other continents. Invite them to come and share with your class.
12. There are so many educational activities you can engage in with your students on the theme of continents. You may want to restrict your continental study to one continent per month. This will give students ample time to get involved in an in-depth study, and to prepare special projects within the classroom setting. The study of the continents alone is tremendous, and this theme allows you to move in any direction that you choose.

Refer to Appendix B to record your own curriculum standards.

OTHER TEACHER-SUGGESTED ACTIVITIES

Activity Thirteen

Pets

PETS BRING SO MUCH JOY AND LOVE to a family. In fact, pets are a part of many families. Just think about the tremendous diversity we have in our homes relating to family pets. There are numerous pets from different species, and an incomprehensible number of pets within a given species. Think of the people who have cats and dogs as pets. One can only imagine the many varieties of other pets. Allow your students to talk about their pets and share the names of their pets. Below are several activities that can enhance and create beneficial real-life experiences about your students' family pets. Get ready for a lively and talkative experience as you enter the diverse world of pets!

OUTLINED SUGGESTED ACTIVITIES

1. Generate a conversation and discussion about diversity by talking about family pets. This should ignite lots of input from students. Probably every student has or once had a family pet. Encourage dialogue and exchange among students.
2. Ask students to talk about their pets. What is special about their pet? Give them specific parameters, or the conversation could definitely go into infinity!
3. Have students select television personalities and share about their pets.
4. Ask students to bring a picture of their pet to class. Part of the discussion should be about how they care for their pet and their responsibilities to ensure that their pet gets proper care.
5. Research: Post pictures of pets in the classroom and select a "Pet of the Week" or "Pet of the Month." During this time, information about the special pet can

be shared. Have students conduct research on the Pet of the Week/Month to find out more about its habits, preferred foods, environment, and so on.
6. List interesting experiences students have encountered with their pets. Examples: rescued from a pet shelter, visited residents of a senior citizens home, or rescued a family member.
7. Work with students on a study of famous pets from television over the years, such as Lassie, Rin Tin Tin, Mr. Ed, Flipper, and more recent pets. What was so unique about each pet?
8. Reading and Research: Through reading, discussing, and studying, what are some of the more unique pets people might have?
9. Social Studies: Study the presidents of the United States and research their pets.
10. Discuss how pets are diverse (food, habitat, behaviors, habits, and care needed). Choose different examples among mammals, fish, birds, reptiles, and amphibians.
11. Mathematics: Once all the students' pets are listed, graph the number of pets per category. Help students color-code different pets. Examples: How many students own dogs, cats, lizards, rabbits, parrots, horses, turtles, and so on?
12. Do you have students in the classroom who have multiple pets? Discuss similarities and differences between the animals. Who has the largest and smallest pets?
13. Invite a veterinarian to come to your class and discuss the care needed for different types of pets. If possible, ask the veterinarian to bring several unusual animals to class for discussion. You may also be able to take a trip to the veterinarian's office.
14. Field Trips: Visit a zoo with your class, and discuss the habitats of animals and their likelihood of being household pets. Compare these habitats. Compare the physical characteristics of the different animals. What does this tell you about the animal? What does it tell you about defense mechanisms? Visit an animal shelter and ask the director to talk about the different types of animals they have, and the types of vaccinations and care necessary to maintain healthy animals.

Refer to Appendix B to record your own curriculum standards.

Other Teacher-Suggested Activities

Activity Fourteen

Languages

LANGUAGE IS ANOTHER AREA WHERE students may differ. This is one aspect of diversity that is on the rise in the American classroom. You may have students who speak different languages. If this is the case, it will present a wonderful opportunity to share with your students the diversity of languages in the world.

As your students embark on the study of various continents, incorporate the study and diversity of the languages. Play songs in various languages in your classroom, and enjoy the richness and diversity.

OUTLINED SUGGESTED ACTIVITIES

1. Social Studies and History: Upper-level elementary students can get involved in the history of languages and a study of many different languages around the world.
2. Are there students in your classroom who speak different languages? Are there staff and faculty members within your school who speak different languages? If so, create activities around the languages. Learning from each other is so important. You might want to have an interpreter come in and discuss and illustrate another language. What are some comparisons students can make regarding different languages? If you have students who speak Spanish, this will be a great opportunity for the class to learn from them and showcase their language. Do you have students who use or know sign language?

3. Label various objects in the classroom in English and the second language, and frequently say them both, allowing students to learn words in a second language.
4. Invite college students who speak another language to visit your school and classroom.
5. Engage in a linguistic study of several countries and continents. Study a few of the languages spoken in different parts of the world.
6. Music: Utilize the expertise of your music teacher. Learn songs in another language.
7. Field Trip: If possible, take the class on a field trip to a restaurant where English is not the primary language.
8. If you have an English-speaking student in your class who is bilingual, have that student assist in organizing the classroom to represent both languages. Examples: English—chair, and Spanish—silla; English—teacher, and Spanish—maestro or profesora.
9. If you are bilingual, integrate your skills into your lessons as you deem appropriate.
10. Research: Conduct research to determine the world's top ten spoken languages, based on estimated population counts for a particular linguistic community. Research some of the primary countries of the world where each language is spoken. Share the vastness of the number of languages with students.

Refer to Appendix B to record your own curriculum standards.

Other Teacher-Suggested Activities

Activity Fifteen

State Flowers/State Trees/State Birds

EACH OF THE FIFTY STATES IN THE United States has adopted a flower to serve as a symbol of that state. A hands-on, research-based study of state flowers can truly be a worthwhile and educational experience for students in the elementary through middle grade levels. Students can share with each other, design their specific flower as a work of art, and, if possible, plant flowers that represent their state on the school campus.

You and your students can decorate the classroom with representations of flowers, trees, and birds of the selected states. Help your students become familiar with the symbols of their native state. This will ignite their curiosity to learn about symbols of the other states. What a great way to learn and gain a better understanding of our world!

OUTLINED SUGGESTED ACTIVITIES

The following are just a few activities that will bring enjoyment, educational awareness, and a great respect for diversity to your students. This theme of state flowers/state trees/state birds will get students outside and in nature to explore the wide range of each symbol.

1. Science and Social Studies: Assign states to students or have them select one state to research such areas as (1) vegetation, (2) seasonal/climatic temperatures, (3) rainfall/precipitation, (4) animal life, (5) state tree, (6) state flower, and (7) state bird. Comparing the states will show tremendous uniqueness and diversity.

2. Science: Depending on the grade level, students can expand their study to areas such as scientific names of adopted state flowers, scientific names of state trees, common names of flowers, and other environmental factors relating to flower and tree growth and development. Discuss seasonal characteristics: when is the adopted state flower in bloom? Can a group of students determine why that flower was selected to represent the state? What are some visible characteristics of the state flower?
3. Have students construct large state maps that include facts such as (a) state capital, (b) primary economic resources, (c) one or two significant landform facts, (d) the state flower, and (e) other information of your choice. Post in the classroom for study and frequent referral.
4. After individual, whole-class, and specific group projects have been completed, have students discuss the wide diversity of state flowers. Are there flowers that are similar in color, size, fragrance, texture, physical appearance? Are there states with the same or similar state flowers? If so, what are their differences and similarities?
5. Geography: Restrict the study of state flowers to a particular locale (five or six southern states, western coastal states, and so on). This will limit your class study and will provide opportunities for further studies of flowers in groups.
6. Language Arts: Develop games and flash cards about states and state flowers. This is a wonderful opportunity to involve students with different learning styles. Give your students an opportunity to develop games. Their input and creativity might pleasantly surprise you.
7. Social Studies: Incorporate a number of state facts into your unique state-flower game. Set up a debate team or competitive game of *Name That State Flower*. This can give rise to lots of fun, yet is a tremendous learning experiences for students. Design your debate or name game as you so desire. Other games may include such areas of study as naming state capitals, the geographical location of a state within the United States, name the state trees, and naming the state birds.
8. Give students an opportunity to make or draw large state flowers and put them on bulletin boards or post on classroom walls. Students can refer to the information, which will also serve as a visible reminder that this area of the curriculum is being studied. Students will love to see their creations posted in the classroom and highlighted by you. There also may be an opportunity to share the work of your students in the school halls, the library, and the cafeteria. Consider making this study a schoolwide event!
9. Music: How about having your class create a "State Flower Song"! This could be great for your many different types of learners. Incorporate historical facts about the state to be studied. Opportunities such as these will give you a chance to reflect on your learners and their preferred learning styles and multiple intelligences, and will allow you to design a process that can

incorporate all learning styles and multiple intelligences to create a unique and powerful State Flower Song. Share the song at an open house for parents and the community.

10. Music: If you have students who can play instruments, have them join in and accompany the class by playing their musical instrument.
11. Language Arts/Reading: Think further about creating state flower stories. This will also lead to lots of creativity for your students. If you teach smaller children, work with them on creating a picture book about their state flower. If you teach upper-level elementary students, expand this possibility.
12. Mathematics: Work with students on math activities where they can compare and contrast the geographical area of each state. Give them an opportunity to research and place the states in descending order of square miles.
13. Science: Develop similar activities for your students as they study the state birds.

Refer to Appendix B to record your own curriculum standards.

Other Teacher-Suggested Activities

Activity Sixteen

Length

Using and understanding units of measurement is an important part of elementary mathematics. It is also vital in learning and understanding our world. Using the theme of length to solve problems and to better understand our surroundings is of paramount importance to ensure that students have the necessary skills to cope well in the twenty-first century. Start with the various length concepts, and work with your students so they can observe that even though units of length, weight, time, and so on are diverse, each has an impact and can build on the other. Without the smaller units, there would not be larger units.

Make sure you have adequate measuring resources and tools for your students to use. Store your rulers, tape measures, yardsticks, and meter sticks in a special location. Encourage students to measure objects and areas around the classroom, and compare the lengths and widths of each. The activities suggested below can be modified to teach other units of measurement as you deem appropriate.

Outlined Suggested Activities

1. Mathematics: Introduce students to the unit of an inch. Use rulers, yardsticks, meter sticks, and so on to show students the length of an inch. Allow students to use rulers and other measuring devices to measure objects in the classroom. Divide students into pairs or groups. Have your students discuss and record their findings as they measure.
2. Expand measurement activities to longer units of length—feet and yards. Continue using the measurement of the inch to show how interconnected the inch

is to feet and yards. Have students measure, measure, and measure. Allow them to continue measuring objects outside the classroom, under your supervision.
3. Technology: Integrate technology into your study. Use Internet activities by way of Smart Boards to interact with students.
4. Art: Direct students as they cut out inch, foot, and yard units in various colors. They can use the color-coded units to compare and contrast. This activity will allow them to see how each connects with the other.
5. As your students progress, move to other units of capacity. Use the following as teaching tools to measure volume:
    - Teaspoon
    - Tablespoon
    - Cup
    - Pint
    - Gallon

    Sand is a great, easily accessible material to use with students to conduct measurement activities. Have students work problems by using the tools above.
6. Mathematics: Introduce students to the concept of mass. Use scales to measure, and teach students the relationship between ounces and pounds, ounce to grams, and so on.
7. Reading and Mathematics: Have students bring in labels from plastic and paper containers with designated mass amounts (liquid and solid). Use some of the labels to measure in class. Demonstrate the measuring process and allow students to directly engage in hands-on activities so that they will become comfortable with measuring different unit capacities.
8. Introduce and demonstrate height. Use tape measures to find the height of students and the teacher in the classroom. Be creative in how you develop this activity. This should increase student involvement, because students enjoy comparing their height with that of their classmates. Closely monitor students as they engage in this high-energy activity. Measure in inches; convert to feet. Make classroom measuring markers decorative and exciting. Use cartoon characters as a part of your decoration for measurement.
9. Tape and mark measurements on the classroom wall in a location where students can conduct measurements of height.
10. Set up a "Math Measuring Center" in your classroom with objects students can measure. Some suggestions are sand, water, colored water, dirt, and small rocks. Make sure this area is secure and well monitored. Give students the responsibility of cleaning up after they work on measuring activities. You may also include within the center some of the following: tape measures, rulers, measuring rods, measuring cups, teaspoons, tablespoons, yardsticks, and other measuring devices. Again, monitor the classroom center for safety and cleanliness. Students tend to spill and drop.

Refer to Appendix B to record your own curriculum standards.

OTHER TEACHER-SUGGESTED ACTIVITIES

Activity Seventeen

Tools

INTRODUCE YOUR STUDENTS TO THE concept of hand tools. Tools are objects used to do a specific job. This theme will hopefully get all of your students up and moving. Every student has some type of experience with tools. An activity that addresses the use of tools is one way to teach diversity.

Each tool is unique in that it serves a specific purpose. If all tools performed the same function, we would have major problems in the home, at school, and everywhere. Tools were invented to solve some type of problem.

OUTLINE SUGGESTED ACTIVITIES

1. Give students an opportunity to share about hand tools they use. Talk about several very familiar hand tools in the home, such as:
   - Wrench
   - Pliers
   - Scissors
   - Bottle opener
   - Flashlight
   - Kitchen strainer
   - Nail file
   - Pencil sharpener

   Talk about several school tools students may frequently use. What purpose does each serve? Caution students about the use of tools. Many should only be used by an adult or in the presence of an adult.

2. Research: Assign students several hand tools to research, and have them bring to class two important facts about these tools. After this activity is completed, have students share their findings.
3. Assign students a project in which they share and compare tools you might find in different environments, such as the home, school, doctor's office, grocery store, barber shop, beauty parlor, and recreation center. Select other settings.
4. Language Arts: Have students write essays on "The Tool We Cannot Do Without." Look for tool facts, and research what students require to prepare essays. Limit the length of the essay as appropriate.
5. History: Conduct research on several commonly used tools and how they have evolved over centuries.
6. Assign students in groups. Have each group prepare a project titled "Tools." Have them present this in class with drawings and models.
7. Technology: Create a PowerPoint presentation on the use of hand tools, explaining the significance and uniqueness of each tool. You may limit these to a short list of commonly used hand tools to increase understanding of the purpose of each tool. Too many tools may create confusion. Select hand tools that students are familiar with, and have observed being used by their parents and in the home environment.
8. Prepare a field trip to the school cafeteria. Work with the cafeteria manager as he or she presents some of the primary tools used in the cafeteria and kitchen to prepare food, and explains the purpose of each tool.
9. Writing: Assign students a creative writing activity. If they could improve a specific tool, which one would they choose, and what would the improvement be?
10. Invite a parent who works with tools, such as an auto mechanic or cosmetologist, to the class to discuss the diversity of the various tools that he or she uses within a day.
11. Research with students some of the latest inventions relating to tool improvements.

Refer to Appendix B to record your own curriculum standards.

Other Teacher-Suggested Activities

Activity Eighteen

Insects

INTRODUCE THE STUDY OF ECOSYSTEMS to your students. As a part of the study, create a scientific environment in which your students can study the relationships of plants to animals, and their interdependence. Have students engage in a study of insects. Go on a virtual field trip or, better still, a field trip around campus collecting and identifying insects. Review the teaching standards and objectives for your grade level in the area of science to appropriately integrate the study of insects into your Other Teacher Suggested Activities page.

OUTLINED SUGGESTED ACTIVITIES

1. Science: Spring is a wonderful time to introduce students to the study of the world of insects. Construct, using the material of your choice, the parts of an insect. Once students see the individual parts, they can better identify them from actual collected samples.
2. Introduce insects to your students by engaging them in conversation. Ask them to name several types of insects. Restrict your study of insects and ecosystems to your immediate environment. What are some of the primary insects found in your area?
3. Continue to restrict the study to a limited number of insects, perhaps four or five. A wider variety can be studied at a later time. Discuss the similarities and differences of these insects.
4. Work with students to determine the role of each insect in the ecosystem of your immediate environment. What types of insects might exist in various

ecosystems, such as swamp, desert, mountains, or beach? Why do these insects live in their particular environment?
5. Art and Science: Draw and display different types of insects. Post this information in your classroom for future reference.
6. Social Studies: Continue your insect study for several states. If time permits, expand your study to several other countries. Observe and discuss the different types of insects prevalent in each area.
7. Field Trip: If it is possible to attend a zoo, visit with your students to see what types of insects are on display to continue studying the world of insects. Students will be able to take some of their knowledge from the classroom to the zoo environment. At the zoo, they will get a picture of how much they have learned already about insects. Now they can take something they have learned from the zoo back into the classroom.
8. Remember, these will be high-energy educational activities, so proceed with caution!

Refer to Appendix B to record your own curriculum standards.

OTHER TEACHER-SUGGESTED ACTIVITIES

Activity Nineteen

Alphabet Letters

COMMUNICATION IS AT THE core of our lives. It is the engine that keeps life moving. Just think about the many verbal/linguistic forms of communication we encounter each day! How could we survive without speaking, writing, reading, listening, and talking? It would be extremely difficult, if not impossible, to function in our society without these forms of communication.

The twenty-six letters of the alphabet are basic to our communication system. The following are just a few of the dynamic activities your students can engage in to learn and better understand our world. Have students think, before engaging in these activities, how difficult it would be to have a breakdown in our twenty-six-letter alphabet. Think of how different the letters are, but how each serves a tremendous purpose in communication. These activities should open up a world of exploration, discovery, and excitement.

OUTLINED SUGGESTED ACTIVITIES

1. All students should be very familiar with the twenty-six letters of the alphabet. They can identify each letter individually and can identify words formed from different letters. Engage students in a variety of reading, writing, and speaking activities.
2. Generate a conversation with students on the differences among letters and how, without even one, communication would be different. Eliminate one of the twenty-six letters each day. This will show the void we might have in our

lives without the selected alphabet letters and the diversity we need in order to communicate effectively.

3. Integrate with all areas. As students go about their daily reading, have them color the alphabet letter that was eliminated that day. This shows how frequently the selected letter is used.
4. Writing: As sentences are developed during class activities, have students complete their written activity and go back and color the letter eliminated that day. Have a sharing session so all students can actually see the impact one letter can have on communication. Some letters will have a significant impact, but all will affect how we communicate with each other and the level of communication. Monitor these activities closely. You do not want to spend too much time on coloring and eliminating letters, but such an activity will allow students to observe the importance of each letter.
5. Collect short newspaper articles. Have students color or cross out a specific letter. Use a variety of newspaper articles: advertisements, local news, world news, announcements, sports and, so on. Place several articles on an overhead projector and work through them, discussing how the elimination of a letter might look and impact the overall meaning of an article.
6. Technology: Use your Smart Board to illustrate similar points as discussed in (6) above.
7. Select one short article for your students. Read together and discuss:

   - What is the article about?
   - After eliminating a letter, rewrite the article as best as possible, trying to maintain the same meaning. Do some words need to be changed? This may be a more difficult activity for younger students. Tailor your activity to meet the needs and levels of your students.

8. Mathematics: Select three or four sentences. List each letter and the number of times each is used in the three or four sentences. Develop math problems around the frequency of usage. Examples: A = 5; E = 12; Y = 2; O = 5, and so on. You can develop activities for fractions, decimals, ratios, percentages, and even colorful graphs to show comparisons.
9. Technology: Engage students in a conversation about the latest technology, and use texting and Twitter as examples. How does this technology impact the use of letters and complete sentences? Are some letters omitted or substituted? Are all texts written in complete sentences?

Refer to Appendix B to record your own curriculum standards.

OTHER TEACHER-SUGGESTED ACTIVITIES

Activity Twenty

Greeting Cards

DIVERSITY OF EXPRESSION IS all around us. Just think of the many different types of greeting cards people send to each other on a daily basis. Students can relate to this activity, because all have at some time received or sent some type of greeting card. Allow them to start off these activities by telling the class what type of cards they have received and what made them so special. Start a lively discussion about the many different types of greeting cards there are, and their significance.

OUTLINED SUGGESTED ACTIVITIES

1. Bring to class several different categories of specialty cards, such as holiday, birthday, marriage, get-well, congratulatory, and thank-you cards.
2. Ask your students to put these cards into specific categories. How many different categories can be made from the cards you shared with your students? Can students think of other kinds of cards that are given on special occasions? Determine the categories for the cards.
3. Language Arts: Integrate this activity into your language arts class. Have your class select six or seven major event categories such as birthday, wedding, holiday (specify), and so on. Work with them as they design wording for the categories they selected. You may want to put students in groups and assign categories to the groups. Students can rotate between groups as they complete categories.
4. Assign each student a category, and have them design verses for the assigned category. Assign students another category. Have them design verses for the

next assigned category. This will give them opportunities to design diverse messages suitable for designated categories of greeting cards.

5. Language Arts/Art: Pair up students and have them design a special greeting card for a special occasion. This should come with pictures and verses. Post them in the classroom.

6. Discuss how class-designed cards are alike, and how they are different. Are there occasions for which we would like to design special cards? If so, what are they? Share some possibilities with students, such as:

- Pet's birthday
- First tooth
- All As on a report card
- Celebration of a "good character" trait
- Ready for summer
- First day of school
- Welcome back to school!

7. Character Education: Work with students on the design of a special classroom card in recognition of character education traits. Establish a "Character Education Week" in your class. Work with students on the final product. Polish and tailor the card so you can reproduce it and give it to a student at the end of each week. This specially designed class card can be signed by you and the school principal. Make this a whole-class activity where all students can participate and achieve some level of success. Discuss the wide range of greeting cards and the purpose of different categories of greeting cards.

Refer to Appendix B to record your own curriculum standards.

OTHER TEACHER-SUGGESTED ACTIVITIES

Activity Twenty-One

Holidays

Holidays are a wonderful theme to teach and illustrate diversity. Everyone is familiar with at least one holiday and also has a favorite holiday. We all celebrate, no matter what our culture, race, religion, or nationality. These are excellent suggestions to get your students involved in sharing about their favorite holiday. It will also open the door to discussion and further research on unfamiliar holidays and their meanings. You can even integrate holiday activities with Activity Two: Months of the Year suggestions to allow your students to research the holidays of each month. Review your months of the year activities and try to create even more powerful ideas as you teach about diversity.

Outlined Suggested Activities

1. Write down four or five of the most popular and most widely celebrated holidays. Ask students to respond. Generate discussion and involvement as you see fit. Some questions to ask include:

    - Are these only holidays we celebrate?
    - What are some favorite holidays, and why?
    - How is each of these different? How are they alike?

2. Conduct a holiday study of each month. What is the significance of each holiday? Study with your students various cultural holidays, such as St. Patrick's Day, Kwanzaa, Chinese New Year, Hanukkah, United Nations Day, Civic Holiday (Canada), and the first day of Ramadan.

3. Research the number of holidays in each month. Some students may find holidays others have missed.
4. Students can also be assigned their birth month to search out holidays.
5. Mathematics: Which month has the most holidays, based on in-depth research?
6. History: Select one holiday each month and have the class study its origin, history, significance, who celebrates it, and so on.
7. Smaller children can select a special holiday, draw the holiday as they see it, and color it. How might Easter look to a child? What colors would represent Easter? Display these holiday representations in the classroom so students can see their works of art.
8. Plan with your students and parents a "Holiday Dress-Up Day." What are the colors represented, special food, special activities, music, art, and so on associated with the holiday?
9. Music: Listen to different holiday songs with your students. Have them develop their holiday songs and share with the class.

Refer to Appendix B to record your own curriculum standards.

Other Teacher-Suggested Activities

Activity Twenty-Two

Sports

STUDYING DIVERSE SPORTS WILL enable you to design lessons around Howard Gardner's theory of the Multiple Intelligences as you work with your students on these activities. Sports-related activities are high energy, and most students easily become actively involved. If you teach students who are not bodily-kinesthetically talented, work in other areas of the multiple intelligences to cover the range of diversity found in sports. Be creative with this theme.

Remember, do your research in this area before teaching. Below are several high-energy activities that can be easily integrated into areas of the curriculum. These introductory activities will enable you to establish the strengths, comfort levels, and even the weaknesses of students in physical education activities. It is okay to discover the weaknesses. We all have them. Once we can pinpoint a weakness, we can begin to alleviate or lessen that weakness.

OUTLINED SUGGESTED ACTIVITIES

1. Physical Education and Health: As a part of your physical education/health program, introduce students to various physical activities that lead to appreciating certain skills such as walking, jumping, running, throwing, catching, skipping, hopping, and dodging. These skills require minimal to substantial physical movement. Take into consideration the various skill levels. Some students may be able to run faster, while others may excel in jumping, walking, or throwing. Work to develop activities that will showcase the strengths of each student. Use a variety of physical activities to get students involved in movement. Be mindful of their abilities.

2. Physical Education: Introduce students to one of the most common yet frequently overlooked forms of meaningful physical education—walking. Take a walk with your students several times around the classroom, in the school gymnasium, or around the school buildings, or go on a nature walk. As students walk, allow them to discuss what they observe, especially on relatively long walks. Try to maintain a steady walking pace. Graduate to more sophisticated forms of movement. Students should be exposed to diverse physical activities. Discuss how each is good for the body. In doing so, students will become involved early on in various physical education activities and appreciate the uniqueness and value of each.
3. Introduce your students to a sport of your choice. Show how physical activities such as walking, running, jumping, hopping, and dodging play into the designated sport.
4. Language Arts: Have students share their favorite sport. Document each. Discuss with students the diversity exhibited in sports as a result of the list. Pair students who selected the same sport. Each pair must:

 - explain the sport
 - name at least two famous people associated with the sport
 - name equipment used for the sport
 - explain why this is their favorite sport
 - List skills needed in order to successfully play this sport

5. Technology: Use a Smart Board and the Internet to discuss at least two popular sports with your students. Emphasize how they differ and how they are similar.
6. Group students who enjoy the same sport. Work with them as they develop a sports rap song. Have the groups present at a designated time. Videotape students' presentations and play them back so they can see and hear their performances.
7. Language Arts: Designate sports commentators to give a recap of special sports events that have occurred on television. Help students with news reports. Invite a sports commentator to class to discuss his or her job responsibilities.
8. Invite professional athletes to your class to talk with students. Have them wear their sports outfits, if appropriate. Invite local high school athletes to act as big buddies to your students. Assign high school athletes as big readers and big mathematicians along with your students. This should take place under your strict supervision.
9. Record, as a class, as many different sports as possible. Post the list on a large chart in the classroom. Talk about diversity as it relates to different equipment used in sports. Discuss specialized training one must undertake in order to play certain sports.

10. Take students on a school-sponsored field trip to a local college, university, or YMCA to observe a sports event.
11. Have students bring to class newspaper or Internet sports articles. Did students bring a variety of articles? Are different sports represented? Continue to talk about the many kinds of sports and the diversity they bring to the world of entertainment. Again, share and discuss sports that your students may be unaware of and research these, such as lacrosse, equine sports, and chess.
12. Health: Research and discuss with students the importance of engaging in physical education and sports activities. Talk about how this can address obesity and other health-related problems young people are now encountering. Gear this activity so that you are comfortable discussing these, and students better understand the need to be involved in physical activity to maintain good health.

Refer to Appendix B to record your own curriculum standards.

Other Teacher-Suggested Activities

Activity Twenty-Three

States and Capitals

HOW MIGHT YOUR STUDENTS VIEW diversity if they were to study the fifty states? The answer: in many different and exciting ways. Each of our fifty states is uniquely beautiful. Many similarities, but also many differences make each state special. Some have mountains, others magnificent lakes, extraordinary plant life, exceptional beaches, and much more.

Engage your students in social studies and geography lessons to bring this diversity to light. Get ready for lots of learning and discovery. Explore, read, research, share, and learn!

OUTLINED SUGGESTED ACTIVITIES

1. Social Studies: Depending on the grade level, start familiarizing students with the states that make up the United States of America. A strong beginning might be to learn more about your state. Continue by weaving information about your home state into a study of other states.
2. Social Studies and Geography: Using a large map of the United States, identify the states. Start off with a few states. Break states down into various geographical regions, such as the southern states, midwestern states, northeastern states, and so on.
3. Study the geography and topography of the various regions. How are they similar? How are they different? What are some major crops grown in each region?
4. Allow students to construct large state maps and develop distinguishable land forms common to each state. Have groups of students research the climate of specific geographical regions and give a report to the class.

5. With assistance from your students, develop flash card games on states and capitals. File the state/capital games in learning centers so that students can periodically return to the center to work independently on game activities.
6. Music and Language Arts: With your students, make an audiotape for classroom use, naming each state and its capital with the correct spelling of each. Have exciting, lively background music on the audiotape.
7. Music and Physical Education: Integrate physical education movements with the state/capital audiotape. Students can help put the movements to music and narration. This will accommodate students of various learning styles and multiple intelligences.
8. Assign students to study groups to conduct research on areas such as, but not limited to:

    - State capital, flower, song, tree, and bird
    - Mammals common to the state
    - Insects common to the state
    - Seasonal temperatures or other state facts
    - State history and famous residents of the state
    - State nickname and the story behind the name
    - Large drawing (map) of the state and the number of square miles of area

9. Establish a state/capital quiz bowl competition for students. Tailor the quiz bowl to meet the needs of your students.
10. Social Studies and Science: Finalize your class study of states by discussing the diversity of names, capitals, temperatures, locations, land formations, vegetation, animals, and other characteristics you have researched and studied.
11. Social Studies: Study the colonies prior to U.S. independence. Divide into the Southern, Middle, and New England colonies.
12. You, along with your students, may also consider making a documentary about the various characteristics of the states. This will allow every child to get involved, participate, and learn.

Refer to Appendix B to record your own curriculum standards.

OTHER TEACHER-SUGGESTED ACTIVITIES

Activity Twenty-Four

Road Signs

TRAVELING UP AND DOWN highways, bypasses, freeways, and even country roads is a part of our everyday existence. Being able to travel—and travel well—depends on many factors, including the availability of accurate road signs. Road signs are an important part of our lives, yet seldom do we stop to think about their value and diversity.

Even though your students do not drive, they travel with parents, grandparents, other family members, and friends. Many even travel back and forth to school on the school bus. Students encounter road signs daily. The suggested activities provide a springboard for you to dive into other significant and meaningful ways to teach about diversity, using simple items that are around us: road signs. Let's jump right into this adventure!

OUTLINED SUGGESTED ACTIVITIES

1. Initiate a classroom conversation about road signs and their purpose. Without sharing your opinions with students, allow them to start off by sharing different types of road signs they have observed. List these on the blackboard, a flip chart, or a Smart Board where students can readily see the names of each. Once the list becomes large, ask students to help you put the road signs into distinct categories of function and purpose. Ask them to explain why all signs are not in the same categories. How might the different categories impact traveling from one point to another?

2. Mathematics: Describe the geometric shapes of some of the road signs, such as stop signs, caution signs, no-U-turn signs, follow the circle, and so on. Discuss points, angles, lines, and other characteristics. Have students identify angles and lines as they discuss the signs. Talk about color, and what a color means with respect to specific categories of signs.
3. Assign groups of students to research specific categories. Give them several weeks to finalize their class report on the many different road signs in a category. Make sure that you review with them where they are and the direction they are moving within this time, for a final report.
4. Language Arts: Provide guidelines for students to develop essays about a town without road signs. What types of problems might result in such a town? Once completed, allow students to read and share their diverse opinions and ideas.
5. Art: Over a period of several weeks, ask students to bring in newspaper and magazine clippings of various types of road signs. Take time during art class to work with your students as they develop a collage of travel with all their road signs represented.
6. Critical Thinking: Take a poll of the number of students in your classroom whose parents travel long distances with GPS systems. How might these travel devices impact the availability of road signs in the future? Where might one find temporary road signs? What are temporary electronic road signs? Why are these signs used?
7. Have students think about and answer the question "If I could be a road sign, what type would I be and why?" Share in class. Discuss the great variety and importance of each sign. Continue to talk with students about what signs they see each day as they travel from home to school.
8. Conclude with thought-provoking discussions with students about the many signs they see in their school, and what these signs mean. Do these signs assist us in finding our way around the school, and in a safer manner? Observe road signs and other signs you might find in other places, such as restaurants, hospitals, and shopping malls. Even though these are not road signs, they help us travel and navigate around specific areas. Continue your study of road signs with other creative strategies.
9. Technology: Work with students on the use of modern-day technology, and research how road signs have been improved as a result of technology. Cite examples of how road sign information may be communicated by way of GPS systems. Discuss relatively new approaches such as Amber and Silver alerts, and how these may be used to warn travelers. Might there be other types of alerts?

Refer to Appendix B to record your own curriculum standards.

Other Teacher-Suggested Activities

Activity Twenty-Five

Systems and Organs of the Body

THE HUMAN BODY IS FASCINATING because of its complex makeup. As you embark on a study of the human body, consider using this theme to teach how diverse yet interdependent our systems and organs are. Every organ and system must work efficiently for the body to be healthy.

Work with your students as they create a replica of the human body with its various systems and organs. This visual, which they take part in creating, will enhance their understanding of the interdependence of bodily systems and organs. When the entire replica is completed, remove an organ and/or system. Ask your students questions about the effect this would have on the functioning of the entire human body.

OUTLINED SUGGESTED ACTIVITIES

1. Health: Introduce students to the major body systems and functions. Discuss some of the major organs of the body. Depending on grade level, some students will be able to name and briefly talk about the function of several of the human body's twenty-two major organs. If students are not familiar with organs and their functions, introduce them to five of the most familiar ones.
2. Technology: Use the Internet and Smart Board activities to make study of the various organs exciting and engaging. Ask a local doctor to come to your class and discuss the body. He or she may even have models of various organs or replicas of the skeletal system to show to students.

3. Art: Students can make organs out of materials you suggest, or they can draw the organs. Making them will be much more fun and hands-on. Establish an "organ center" in your classroom to display the work of the students.
4. Introduce students to one body system at a time, emphasizing its organs. Take time to make sure students understand the function of each system studied. Some literature suggests there are up to eleven systems in the body. Follow your curriculum guide and textbook. Which organs are a part of each system studied?
5. Have students trace a large human body. Put selected organs on the outlined figure by drawing or by making organs out of styrofoam, papier mâché, cloth, or any other material of your choice.
6. Assign teams of students different systems to research, draw, and mount in the classroom.
7. Develop a system-organ game in which students must match the organ with the system, or the system with the organ. Use a Smart Board to teach about the systems of the human body. Work with students as they develop flashcard activities and questions.
8. Technology: Use websites such as KidsKonnect to teach about organs and systems. If you have the opportunity to research educational websites where students can explore, allow them to have fun with the iPads and laptops!
9. Throughout the study of the organs and systems, bring out the unique diversity of each system and organ and how these all work together to keep the human body fit and healthy.

Refer to Appendix B to record your own curriculum standards.

Other Teacher-Suggested Activities

Activity Twenty-Six

Weather Conditions

WE ALL LOVE SUNNY DAYS. But what if the sun was always shining? Or, what if it rained day after day? We usually do not think about the effect of weather conditions on our lives, until we have planned a special activity and the weather forces a change in plans. The activities for weather conditions present a dynamic opportunity to study the impact and importance of diverse weather conditions.

As the teacher, you can move these activities into many different directions with lively discussion, critical-thinking skills, and creativity. Activities can be incorporated into science, health, social studies, language arts, and technology. Be creative! Remember to review teaching standards for your particular grade level and content area. Explore and enjoy!

OUTLINED SUGGESTED ACTIVITIES

1. Embark first on a study and discussion of climate and weather. Plot weekly meteorological conditions on a classroom weather report board that can be seen by all students. Have students take turns posting weather information. This will give everyone an opportunity to get involved. Plotting conditions daily will encourage students to watch the weather report on television or on their electronic devices. A study of the local weather conditions is very important at this stage.
2. Mathematics: Plotting weather conditions will afford you an excellent opportunity to have students develop math problems about the weather,

through questions such as: How much warmer is the temperature today than it was yesterday?
3. Technology and Social Studies: Have students go online and research weather forecasts for your local area. Next, have students do the same for other areas being studied, both nationally and internationally.
4. Social Studies: Design an assignment for a daily comparative study of the weather (example: Baltimore, Maryland, and London, England). Students will be able to see a contrast and will better understand that weather conditions vary from place to place. This is an excellent lesson on diversity.
5. Have students discuss weather, complete reports, and research weather conditions such as:

- Rainy weather
- Cold weather
- Breezy weather
- Hot temperatures

What are some of the positives and negatives of weather conditions? Why are diverse weather conditions necessary? Integrate plant growth and development, pollination, insects, and so on into the classroom study. Create science lessons around these topics.

6. Discuss the four seasons. What are some of the major weather conditions of each season in your part of the United States? As your students embark on the seasons of the year, work with them as they set up the classroom to reflect the most common weather conditions of that season.
7. Science: Develop projects on global warming and what it means. Does it have an impact on the seasonal changes? What does research reveal?
8. Language Arts: If students were given an opportunity to represent each season with a color, what would that color be, and why? Have students write an essay answering these questions. Have students represent weather conditions by colors. Why were these colors selected? Do different students select different colors for the same weather conditions? If so, why?
9. Invite a meteorologist to visit the classroom and discuss weather conditions and meteorological terms with the students. Invite them during weather-specific times of the year, for example, during tornado season.
10. Field Trip: Take a field trip to the local weather station and meet with the weather team. View weather-forecasting equipment and talk about how the equipment gathers weather-related information. Have the weather team share the latest in computer technology and how they forecast the weather.
11. If your area has a weather van, ask the weather van to visit your school and talk to your class about the special equipment on the van used to collect data and transmit information to a weather station or television studio.

12. History: Help students study the history of weather predicting and how it has changed over the last fifty or so years. Research the changes in the types of equipment over the years.
13. Integrate the use of graphic organizers to help students learn about various types of weather conditions. These visuals will help students observe, organize, and comprehend concepts.

Refer to Appendix B to record your own curriculum standards.

Other Teacher-Suggested Activities

Activity Twenty-Seven

Shoes

START WITH A GENERAL CONVERSATION about what it means to be diverse. Introduce a commonly known item to your students—shoes—to inspire and ignite wonderful activities and conversation. What types of shoes do we wear? Are they the same for all types of weather conditions, events, or activities? Get your students thinking about the many different types of shoes worn by people.

Incorporate similar activities with the study of the continents. Do people on different continents wear the same types of shoes? If not, why is this the case? Why might shoes be different from country to country and continent to continent?

OUTLINED SUGGESTED ACTIVITIES

1. Social Studies: Start with a study of cultural groups. Include cultural traditions such as food, clothing, shelter, holidays, dance, and music. Select several groups with your class, such as:

   - Native American
   - Hispanic
   - Chinese
   - Russian
   - Inuit
   - Dutch

2. Integrate a study of the primary types of shoes worn by the groups studied. Have your students research reasons why specific cultures wear different

types of shoes. Could terrain or environment play a major role? Are there people who do not wear shoes?
3. Art: Have students draw or make shoes worn by different cultures. If people from different cultures live in your community, invite them to come to your classroom and discuss their native dress, particularly the types of shoes worn by their culture.
4. Work with students on developing a large "tree of shoes" reflecting various cultures, and display it in the classroom.
5. Have students discuss the many types of shoes they have at home. Which shoes are worn for which occasions? Have shoes changed over the years for men, women, boys, and girls? If so, why and how?
6. Work with students as they establish categories of shoes. Discuss the diversity of categories. Several might be:

- Sports (designate the sport: baseball, track and field, lacrosse, dance, etc.)
- Formal wear
- House shoes/slippers
- Casual wear

7. Language Arts: Students can individually select a shoe of their choice and write a short narrative on why this is their favorite shoe. Have them read and share with classmates.
8. Language Arts and Reading: Select several children's stories. Have students talk about the different types of shoes worn by characters in each of the stories. Open a discussion about the stories and the shoes.

Refer to Appendix B to record your own curriculum standards.

Other Teacher-Suggested Activities

Activity Twenty-Eight

Planets

THE SCIENTIFIC STUDY OF THE eight planets will bring to your classroom a higher level of understanding as well as appreciation for planetary diversity. Implement these activities as a part of the study of planets. Have your students conduct research. What is the status of Pluto? Is there evidence of other planets? What are the characteristics of the planets? How are they similar, and how do they differ? Transform your classroom into a delightful and educational solar system environment. Study some of the latest research as it relates to planetary discoveries.

OUTLINED SUGGESTED ACTIVITIES

1. Science: As students engage in a study of planets, what they consist of and other aspects, watch a video or DVD about the characteristics of each planet. The planets represent a vast array of diversity.
2. Research *Discovery Channel* information on planets to share with your students, and watch shows together.
3. Look at how the planets are classified. They are categorized primarily based on their surface atmospheric makeup (solid rock vs. gases). This is another level of diversity. What are the characteristics of the rocky planets? How are they different from the gas planets?
4. Divide students into two groups for study and research on the planets. You can team teach with your school's media specialist to provide a technology presentation on the planets. The media specialist can reinforce what you are teaching in the science classroom.

5. Art: Team teach with the art teacher. Studying the planets in conjunction with creating planetary models will spark a higher level of interest and learning.
6. Field Trip: If possible, take students on a field trip to a local science museum or to a planetarium.
7. Set up a learning center of the solar system in your classroom. Prepare a scientifically accurate solar system model that students can view, close up. Along with this hands-on model, help students construct their own models of the planets and solar system.
8. Work with the class to facilitate the study of different aspects of planets, such as:

   - Size
   - Temperature
   - Distance from the sun
   - Surface characteristics
   - Atmospheric makeup
   - Other physical/chemical attributes

9. Present to your students an historical account of the planets. Discuss the status of Pluto. Have other planets been discovered? Integrate into your study the most recent updates about the solar system.
10. Online Research: Find websites that students can explore with their iPads and laptops to find up-to-date facts on the planets.

Refer to Appendix B to record your own curriculum standards.

OTHER TEACHER-SUGGESTED ACTIVITIES

Activity Twenty-Nine

Modes of Transportation

THE ABILITY TO MOVE FROM one location to another varies from person to person. Every day, many of us use several different modes of transportation. Think how difficult life would be if we did not have different ways to move from place to place.

What were some of the first modes of travel? How did earlier ways of traveling impact today's transportation systems? What are some of the latest ways that people move about from place to place? Get your students involved in critical thinking, and "thinking outside the box." Predict transportation possibilities for the future. Below are just a few activities to enhance this aspect of diversity. Use these activities to generate many more. All are excellent ways to understand our world.

OUTLINED TEACHER SUGGESTED ACTIVITIES

1. Start with a general conversation about and definition of modes of transportation to ensure each student will have an opportunity to share from personal experience. Rich discussion and conversation teach students to listen, respond, give personal reflections, and can be a springboard for capturing creativity and imagination. Ask questions such as:

   - What are some of the ways you have traveled back and forth to school this week?
   - How many different modes of transportation have you observed today?
   - What was your first means of transportation?

   Confine the discussion of transportation modes to the students' immediate community environment. There will be room to expand discussion later.

2. Literature: As a part of your class discussion and study, read several children's books that illustrate ways of moving from one location to another. This will be one way of introducing and discussing diversity as it relates to transportation. Stories that may be used to spark discussion on transportation include:

   - Little Red Riding Hood
   - Three Billy Goats Gruff
   - The Three Little Pigs
   - Cinderella
   - Paddle-to-the Sea
   - The Many Adventures of Robin Hood
   - Small Star and the Mud Pony

   Work with students as they read a story and convert the modes of transportation to other ways of being mobile. (Example: Cinderella rides on a motorcycle instead of in a carriage.) How might these changes impact the outcome of the stories?

3. Brainstorm with students on categories of transportation. Discuss transportation on land, in the air, and on water so that students can classify various modes of transportation.

4. Use graphic organizers to help students put transportation types into categories. Have students develop their own unique graphic organizers as they brainstorm. Working with each other will make this more exciting and rewarding.

5. History and Social Studies: Study different cultures and different times in history. Explore the types of transportation used by a particular culture or during a designated time in history. This will allow students to study a historical undertaking of the types of transportation used. Why and how has transportation changed over time? Is there a mode of transportation that has undergone very little change over the last one hundred years?

6. Have students conduct independent research and bring in pictures of unusual methods of transportation. Discuss and post in the classroom. Work with students as they develop a "Transportation Display Book" with examples filed in it. Are there extremely unusual modes of transportation that students discovered as a result of their research?

7. Invite community members to visit the class to be interviewed by teams of students. Have your students prepare a set of questions so that the questions for the different participants are similar. Students can record the responses from the visitors. Invite community members who move around by different means of transport, such as:

   - Runner or jogger
   - Bicyclist
   - Race car driver
   - Emergency vehicle driver

- Fire truck driver
- Airline pilot
- Boat operator

8. Invite a senior citizen to talk with students about how they moved from place to place fifty or more years ago. Encourage students to ask them questions about how they feel about today's transportation modes.
9. Talk with your students about the need for diversity when it comes to traveling and moving from one location to another. Talk about the changes in our scope of movement. Today, people travel easily from country to country. Years ago, this was much more difficult.
10. Work with students on a research project on old forms of transportation. Select a time in history to research.

Refer to Appendix B to record your own curriculum standards.

Other Teacher-Suggested Activities

Activity Thirty

Rocks

AT FIRST GLANCE, A ROCK LOOKS LIKE any other rock. But each has its own history and diversity in makeup and composition. As you engage your students in a study of the formation of rocks, start first with simple collection of rocks in your immediate community or school environment.

There exists tremendous diversity in the types of rocks, their hardness, color, origin, texture, and overall appearance. Students can learn a lot about rock types, their formation, and where different types are located. A series of simple rock tests can be performed in your classroom science laboratory. What fun it will be to examine rocks that are right outside your back door.

OUTLINED SUGGESTED ACTIVITIES

1. Science: Introduce the rock study by sharing several rocks with your class. Ask students to first give a physical description of each. Have several students record these physical differences on the blackboard or Smart Board.
2. Science: Direct and facilitate activities as students use various objects such as fingernails, nails, coins, and so on to scratch and test each rock. Monitor this process very closely. This will help to determine the level of "hardness" of each rock. Have students separate rocks by color. Have students label each rock and record on a chart the color, texture, and hardness as determined from testing.
3. Discuss the ways rocks can be formed. Describe and give examples of sedimentary, igneous, and metamorphic rocks. Use charts, graphs, videos, and so

on to show the differences in the rocks by providing visuals. Utilize a rock-sample kit to help students see the differences. Where do the different types of rocks form? Extend the classroom study to volcanoes. Study the history of rock formation in volcanoes throughout the world. Utilize map study skills to pinpoint the various locations.
4. Technology: Use websites to study rock cycles. Use Smart Board activities to continue the study of rocks. Be sure to explain and discuss the characteristics of each of the three rock types. Select educational DVDs and videos to show to your students throughout this study.
5. Field Trip: Take students on a field trip and put them in teams to collect rocks. Give each group physical characteristics they are to look for as they collect. This will keep students focused on specifics instead of just picking up any type of rock. Limit teams to no more than ten or twelve rocks. Too many rocks may present problems.
6. Share with teams specific information they will need to record as they collect their samples, such as rock size (nickel or quarter size, etc.) color, texture, and other physical characteristics. Once students return to class, set up team labs for them to continue to study rocks. Have students sort rocks by characteristics. They will be able to both observe and appreciate the diversity of their rocks.
7. Once teams have organized their rocks, consolidate teams to sort and compare. Organize this activity as you deem appropriate. Remember, you are now working with a larger group of students with many rocks. Monitor, monitor, and continue to monitor.
8. Science: Direct students to sort and discuss the differences they have observed. Integrate this field trip excursion with the study of metamorphic, igneous, and sedimentary rocks. What does this variety of different rocks tell us about the earth?
9. Mathematics: Develop math problems around your rock study. Students will be able to count, compare, and perhaps even graph the differences. Continue to expand and grow your rock study project.
10. Geology and Science: Collaborate with a local college or university. Invite a professor or students majoring in geology to come to your class and discuss the formation of rocks. Ask the university students to bring rock samples with them.
11. Field Trip: Plan a trip to your local college campus and visit the geology department. This department will probably have an excellent display of rocks and other artifacts that would benefit your students. Geology majors can pair up with your students and continue testing rocks for various identifying factors. Monitor this process with your students very closely.

Refer to Appendix B to record your own curriculum standards.

Other Teacher-Suggested Activities

Activity Thirty-One

Emotions

AS HUMAN BEINGS, WE EXPERIENCE different emotions or feelings. What are these emotions, and why do we feel them? What do they mean? Are emotions a way of protecting us from harm and danger? A study of the different human emotions that are a part of us would be a meaningful part of your health classes. If we can better understand our emotions, we can better understand ourselves, as well as others. Get your class involved in a study of human emotions and discuss their meaning, their differences, and their complexity.

OUTLINED SUGGESTED ACTIVITIES

1. Health: Describe to your class what emotions are. Encourage students to get involved in the conversation so that you will be able to assess the level of understanding of all your students as it relates to emotions. Once you comfortably feel that students have reached a deeper level of understanding about emotions, continue with the activities.
2. A list of human emotions can become quite long. Therefore, limit the types of emotions you cover. Share in class discussions how diverse our emotions are, and how they change from day to day and even minute to minute. After a detailed sharing of information, develop activities surrounding the diversity of human emotions.
3. Have students write down eight to ten emotions they feel are most important. Review all lists and determine the five most basic emotions from the com-

bined lists. Talk about our emotions being a part of human existence. Give examples, which could include:

- Anger
- Disappointment
- Happiness
- Sadness
- Grief
- Fear
- Love
- Gratitude

4. Language Arts: Select and read several children's books. Have students discuss and assign emotions to each main character. How do the characters manage these emotions? Ask students to discuss how they might manage the emotions if they were characters in the story. Some examples: "The Tortoise and the Hare," "Little Red Riding Hood," "The Three Little Pigs," *Love You Forever*, *A Christmas Carol*.
5. Assign emotions to your students or have students select a particular emotion. Ask them to give an example of what triggered a specific emotion they experienced. Share your emotions and talk about what sparks them; for example, *embarrassment* might be caused by going to the grocery store, putting all your groceries in a shopping cart, and discovering that after all your items have been rung up at the register, with a long line of customers behind you, that you forgot your wallet. This will certainly encourage students to get involved in the classroom discussion and share about their own personal experiences.
6. Art: Have students draw their favorite and least favorite emotion. How would these emotions look, expressed in art?
7. Discuss favorite cartoon characters. What emotions do they express? (Examples: Barney, Elmo, Dora, Miss Piggy, the characters in *Frozen*.)
8. Have students work together and bring in newspaper clippings that depict people expressing different emotions. Have them assign an emotion to the facial/bodily expression.
9. Watch an educational or holiday video. Make sure your video is appropriate for this activity. Afford students the opportunity to discuss the characters and assign specific emotions to the characters. Why did certain characters embrace certain emotions? What if each character portrayed the same emotion? How might that impact the program?

Refer to Appendix B to record your own curriculum standards.

Other Teacher-Suggested Activities

Activity Thirty-Two

Types of Sentences

ORAL AND WRITTEN EXPRESSION ARE effective means of communicating with others. It is extremely important for students to be able to effectively communicate. Although electronic and digital technology is all around us, and increasingly being mastered by students, the need to use English correctly in well-structured sentences has not changed. Its mastery is vital to success in life.

As you embark on a study of sentences, it is important for students to understand that not all sentences are the same. Each has special characteristics. Sentences also perform certain functions and have specific purposes. Early instruction on the diversity and purpose of different sentence types teaches students to identify the four basic types of sentences, create the four sentence types, and know when to use each. Below are a few activities that will assist you in teaching the importance and need for diversity as it relates to writing and communicating.

OUTLINED SUGGESTED ACTIVITIES

1. Introduce students to the basic sentence types: declarative, imperative, exclamatory, and interrogative. Work through one basic type before moving to another. Make sure students have gained a thorough understanding of each type. Assign pairs of students a specific type of sentence to write.
2. Physical Education: Reinforce your study of the four sentence types by composing basic sentences that require a degree of physical movement. If students can see it and feel it, they can comprehend it. Some examples: "I looked down beside my foot and saw a snake!" (exclamatory sentence), and "Why is

she so sad?" (interrogative sentence). What kinds of bodily movements could demonstrate the meaning of these sentences?

3. Decide on one common theme and develop the four basic sentence types around the theme. Continue this process until students are comfortable. Assign students to four groups, with each group representing a basic sentence type. Select a theme and have each group compose a sentence with their assigned sentence type. Share and discuss each of the four types.

4. Continue to develop sentence activities, moving from students acquiring knowledge to developing higher level thinking skills such as synthesizing and creating. These activities should help students create, compose, develop, and design independently. For example, ask students to create a short story on a selected theme, such as in science, using only declarative sentences. Then use the same theme and integrate the four basic sentence types throughout the short story. How does this change and improve the meaning of the story? Demonstrate by using eight or ten sentences of the same type, and then using the four different sentence types.

5. Language Arts: Have students select their favorite read-aloud story. Take sentences from the story and discuss the sentence types. What makes each sentence the type it is?

6. Select short news articles. Compare and contrast sentence types. Have students take an article and attempt to rewrite it, using only one or two sentence types. Does this change the meaning of the article?

7. Language Arts: Assign students the task of writing a short essay on a selected topic using the four basic sentence types. After each sentence, give the sentence type and discuss its importance. What difficulties might be encountered by using only one or two sentence types? Would this have an impact on the meaning of the article?

8. Language Arts and Speech: Demonstrate to students what it would be like if we communicated with each other by using only one or two sentence types. Attempt to communicate with your students for five minutes (time yourself) using only imperative sentences or a sentence type of your choice. Discuss afterward the difficulty of effectively communicating in this way. When students feel comfortable, work with them as they attempt to communicate by using one or two sentence types. At this point, students should be able to see, hear, and feel the need for the diverse sentence types.

9. Music: Have students compose a "basic four rap." As part of their rap, require the name of the sentence type at the end of each sentence. Assign students a theme for this activity, such as our new president, the greatest sport of all time, and/or themes selected by the students. Make sure you give them specific guidelines, and watch creativity take off!

10. For younger students, design a puppet show around the four basic sentence types. Use four puppets, one for each sentence type. Call on some of your

parents to assist in making costumes for the puppets. Have students help with the props and stage arrangements. Students can also help to write the script for the puppet show. Name your sentences: Mr. Interrogative, Imperative Bessie, Exclamatory Willie, Declarative Sally, or any names selected by your students. Be creative and have fun with your students. These activities are excellent for Learning and Understanding Our World.

Refer to Appendix B to record your own curriculum standards.

Other Teacher-Suggested Activities

Activity Thirty-Three

Presidents of the United States

A POWERFUL PART OF OUR RICH HISTORY is the executive branch of government, and our U.S. presidents. As your students learn about the United States, design activities that will engage them in the diversity of our presidents.

The following suggested activities will provide a springboard for even more exciting and challenging activities that will embrace diversity. It is important to convey that our country would not have its rich and wonderful history without the diversity of experiences, political affiliation, beliefs, and ideas each president has brought, and will continue to bring, to the office of the president of the United States of America.

OUTLINED SUGGESTED ACTIVITIES

1. Engage students in a conversation about the commander-in-chief. Talk about the news and current events. This will give all of your students an opportunity to research information that is current and relevant. Much of the information students will bring in and share with the class is a result of their direct experiences. They are actually seeing and hearing about the president. Center much of your conversation on how the presidency impacts education. What laws relating to education are in effect? Does the president visit schools and talk about education? If you have students that have visited Washington, DC, did they see the White House?
2. Social Studies: Start off your study by introducing students to what the office of the president means to the history of our country. Have them share

what they know. Research and find a DVD or video on the executive branch of government with information about the responsibilities of the president. Students can also study the executive branch by researching on their iPads.

3. Social Studies: There is a vast amount of information one can study as we research our presidents. Post a chart of our presidents in class. Establish categories of study such as name of the president, years in office, birthplace, state represented, party represented, and several significant contributions during the president's administration. Provide an in-depth study of five to eight presidents at a time. Decide if you want to cover all presidents; you may want to cover the last ten or so. It is important to make students aware of all the presidents, if possible, because each has contributed greatly to our history.

4. Work with students on a detailed study of each, or a certain number of presidents. Establish research categories that may be of interest to your students, such as the number of children they had, or their pets and the names of the pets. Your students may also give you some ideas about specific points to research.

5. Mathematics: Develop math problems about the presidents, such as the most years served versus the least amount of years served; or comparing and contrasting problems, such as comparing states represented by the most presidents to those with the fewest presidents.

6. Develop with your students a "Name this President" game similar to Jeopardy. Have students give suggestions for the makeup of this game of facts. Make sure you study facts and other information on the presidents before completing this exciting game.

7. Art, Social Studies, and Geography: Work with your students as they construct a large map of the United States. Add the names of the presidents to their respective birth states. Other facts about the presidents can be placed in the state. Be flexible with this activity; a lot can be integrated in this particular presidential activity. Once the map of the United States has been created and the names of the presidents inserted in the proper states, talk about what you see. What type of diversity can one see from what has been placed on the map? Continue to talk with students about what they would like to see in terms of an expansion of the diversity regarding the presidents. Are all states represented by a president?

8. President's Day: Create with students a President's Day activity. If that day is a school holiday, select a day when students can come in dressed like their favorite president or prepare a mini-skit about their favorite president based on what they have learned. Make sure you have a variety of presidents represented. Invite a representative from local or state government to come in and talk with students and connect their comments with President's Day and its significance.

9. Role Play: Work with students as they role play several presidents by sharing some of their historical contributions in their speeches and dressing according to that time in history. As the teacher, be involved in the role playing. Videotape presentations if permissible. Invite parents in to see the culminating presentations on the presidents.

Refer to Appendix B to record your own curriculum standards.

OTHER TEACHER-SUGGESTED ACTIVITIES

Activity Thirty-Four

Multiple Intelligences

THIS ACTIVITY ON TEACHING DIVERSITY has been added to the teacher's resource guide to help teachers more effectively teach different content to all children. Students come to us with different experiences, backgrounds, and talents. We now know that all students do not learn in the same way. It is important for us to teach with this in mind.

Howard Gardner pioneered and shared with the world his research on how human beings learn. This information is immensely important to teachers as we teach students and explore different ways of presenting the assigned themes. Gardner's work is worthy of review and consideration as we teach our diverse student population. As you prepare to teach your specific goals, objectives, and themes, consider the multiple intelligence strengths of every child.

OUTLINED SUGGESTED ACTIVITIES

1. Select a theme, such as "various communities of our environment."
2. Look at the goals and objectives you are going to teach.
3. In doing so, design learning activities that will embrace each of the multiple intelligences, which should address every learner in your classroom. You do not have to use each of them for every lesson, but aim to teach so that each child can experience a degree of success. The following multiple intelligences are listed for your convenience and further research:

   - Verbal-linguistic
   - Logical-mathematical

- Musical
- Bodily-kinesthetic
- Interpersonal
- Intrapersonal
- Visual-spatial
- Naturalistic

Your students will learn what is being taught if you implement one or more of the intelligences and teaching approaches.

4. Design activities around the theme of communities of our environment for children who learn best from the verbal-linguistic, musical, or intrapersonal approaches, and so on. As the teacher, view the video or DVD of *Child Prodigies*, which highlights students who are gifted with several of the intelligences. Research other prodigies that you may want to introduce to your students. *Child Prodigies* is a relatively old production, but it gives an excellent depiction of the multiple intelligences and what helps each type of learner best learn.
5. Study how you are going to present your themes as you teach. Integrate as many activities addressing each of the multiple intelligences as possible, while teaching the required content. For this, you will have to know the strengths of all of your students as well as their weaknesses. Continue on a weekly basis with this type of teaching approach as you use multiple intelligences to teach content.

Refer to Appendix B to record your own curriculum standards.

Other Teacher-Suggested Activities

Activity Thirty-Five

Names

This is an activity that will increase student discussion, input, and understanding of diversity. Consider names of people, countries, towns, foods, schools, automobiles, and so on. What is the need for diversity as we talk about names of whatever the subject may be? This may seem insignificant at first glance, but think about the wide range of expression required to make sure we have adequately identified the proper person, food, car, location, or name brands. When it comes to names, there is a tremendous need for diversity to establish accuracy.

Outlined Suggested Activities

1. Start with a discussion of student names. Ask students to give the first name of everyone living in their home. Are the names the same? Are they different? Is it difficult to communicate with a particular person in the home? Continue a discussion about the diversity of names in the home. This is a frame of reference with which any student can relate and identify.
2. Students may be able to discover, by way of research, households where the children or numerous family members have the same name.
3. List the names of your students on the board in your classroom. Students can become engaged in this activity by writing their own names on the Smart Board or blackboard so that the names are visible to all. Concentrate on first names. Are any names the same? If so, are they spelled the same? If names are spelled the same or similarly, is the pronunciation the same? What are some similarities and differences?

4. Are there students in your school with the same first or last names? Do students know other students or adults who have the same name as others in the community?
5. Language Arts: Have students recreate a story and give all the characters the same name. Does this make the interpretation of the story difficult? As the teacher, rewrite a well-known children's story with the same-name characters, and read it to your students. What if all the players on a basketball team were named Michael Jordan? Discuss.
6. Involve students in the need for diversity so that one can differentiate between one person and another, one place versus another, or one town versus another town.
7. Technology: Share with students the name of a particular city or town. Allow them to research the city or town. Are there other cities/towns with the same name as the town they are studying? (Example: Fayetteville, Lexington, and so on).
8. Language Arts: Introduce students to several groups of commonly used words that are spelled differently but pronounced the same. Does this present difficulties in comprehension? Some examples are:

    - Be/Bee
    - Affect/Effect
    - Sale/Sail
    - Pain/Pane

9. Music: Create with your students a "Name Song" that incorporates everyone's first name. Help students set a rhythm to the song. Redo the song by developing different lyrics, rhythm, and rhyme. How do the differences in arrangement give different meanings?
10. History: Conduct a history of names. Have each student research the meaning of their names. You might also research last names if you so desire.
11. Research the names of famous people selected by the students in your class. Keep the list short. Share and discuss.
12. Consider name activities on themes such as:

    - Schools
    - Colleges and universities
    - Name brands for shoes
    - Highways
    - Basketball teams
    - Streets
    - Countries and continents
    - Names of pets

Refer to Appendix B to record your own curriculum standards.

OTHER TEACHER-SUGGESTED ACTIVITIES

Activity Thirty-Six

Stores

A HEALTHY DISCUSSION ABOUT various types of retail stores is another way you can engage your students in sharing and enhance learning and understanding our world. This is one of your goals: to empower every child to provide input and not feel left out of this dynamic learning opportunity.

When we explore diversity, we can gain so much insight on its importance by looking at and valuing those objects and places right around us. Use this theme to spark other ideas as well as to integrate diversity into the curriculum. You may have students from other cultures, and their experiences may be different from many other students. They may be able to enlighten the class on other types of stores that we may not be familiar with in our environment and culture.

OUTLINED SUGGESTED ACTIVITIES

1. Introduce students to diversity relating to different store specialties. First ask students to share categories of different types of retail stores, such as:

    - Grocery
    - Hardware
    - Pharmacy
    - Clothing

    You may want to begin by sharing several categories to give students a jump start. Remember, your list can become quite long, but that is okay. With this approach, students can see the large selection and diversity of retail stores.

2. Have each student bring in at least three pictures of items used in their home. Give them several days to complete their picture selection and bring their selections to class. Once pictures are brought to class, give students the task of assembling the pictures into categories. They should be able to easily sort pictures into categories such as grocery, furniture, pharmacy, baby supply, hair supply, and so on. Limit the number of pictures students bring in, or you will have too many.
3. Mathematics: You may want to set up specific "store centers" in your classroom and integrate math activities as students purchase items from these stores. This could open up a wide range of educational activities—counting money, preparing a dinner menu, or following a budget, to name only a few. Be creative in designing activities.
4. If possible, take a field trip through your town or city to observe and discuss the different types of stores. Have students discuss the value that many stores provide to the community.
5. Technology: Discuss how shopping at various stores has changed over the years. Some students may be familiar with online shopping as they observe their parents.
6. After a study of different stores, begin a discussion about stores that service and provide multiple products, such as Walmart, Lowes, Fresh Market, and so on. Some stores now have sections for food, pharmacy, eye care, laundromats, and even healthcare. There may be stores that also provide other services to shoppers.
7. History: Start a research project on several stores, how they began and why, and the pioneers who founded these businesses.
8. Creative Thinking: Have students design a store of their own. What specialties might this store have, and why? Could your store be a combination of several stores? What value to society might this store serve? Give an example, such as Petco, which offers pet supplies, and pet food, pet grooming and veterinarian services, and information on pet-sitting services.
9. Continue to create even more activities relating to retail stores. Students may also be able to share interesting and productive learning activities.

Refer to Appendix B to record your own curriculum standards.

Other Teacher-Suggested Activities

Activity Thirty-Seven

Addresses

It is very important for younger children to know and be able to articulate their physical address. An address basically describes where one lives or resides. If children get lost, they should be able to share the address of the location where they live with a caring adult such as a teacher or police officer. Work with your students on this basic knowledge. You will find that this theme will shed light on diversity and will enable you to teach the need for diversity through the theme of addresses.

If you are working with older elementary students, your approach to activities around this theme may be somewhat different. No matter what age level, the introduction to and study of addresses in terms of diversity can be beneficial and exciting.

Outlined Suggested Activities

1. Generally introduce and discuss "where places are" with your students by identifying the address. Begin with the school. All your students will be able to relate to the school. Share the specific address that pinpoints the exact location of your school. For example:

    May-Mary Henry Elementary School
    1604 Yellow Elf Leak Street
    Mobile, Alabama 00000

    Discuss each part of the physical address and its meaning to the total address. Now have students compare their home address to the school address. Each student will probably enjoy sharing.

2. As students share their personal addresses, record every variation: street, boulevard, center, court, road, or apartment. Note: You know your students. Make sure you know where each resides. It is not our goal to embarrass any child. What if you have a homeless child in your class? Be mindful of students' feelings and differences when it comes to homes and locations.
3. Social Studies: Conduct a study at a level you deem appropriate for famous buildings, museums, and homes in your city or town. Research their addresses. Move, as you see fit, to addresses of famous places within your state, country, or other countries.
4. Geography: This is an excellent time to integrate map study into your diversity theme. Share specific addresses and locate these on the map or globe, specifying states, cities, and countries. Conduct a study of various locations within certain regions of the United States, such as southern states, midwestern states, Pacific Coast states, and so on.
5. Mathematics and Social Studies: Pinpoint certain addresses and their latitude and longitude readings on the map. Mathematically determine the highest and lowest elevations. Use the mile scale on a map to estimate distance from one address to another.
6. Language Arts: After an in-depth study of the importance of addresses, assign students to small brainstorming/writing groups. Assign the following task: "Write an essay or short story about a city you created, with stores, hospitals, homes, post offices, doctor offices, and businesses. The problem is that there are no addresses for any of the locations. How might people survive and/or thrive in an environment without addresses of any kind?" Your students may give different responses—expressions of diverse views and interpretations.
7. Critical Thinking: After students have spent sufficient time on group work, brainstorming, researching, and assembling their final product, have them present their creations. Talk about each. Introduce another perspective to stimulate a thought-provoking discussion. What might be some of the features of a community with the same address for every residence and building? What are some problems that can be identified and why?
8. This may appear to be an unlikely theme for a study of diversity, but it is quite the opposite. This theme can truly invoke creativity, lots of discussion, brainstorming, and a deeper level of appreciation for diversity. It would be interesting to see how a group of adults would respond and react to this same theme. Continue to emphasize the need to know specific addresses.
9. Technology and Mathematics: Get students involved in estimating distances by using a GPS on their iPads or laptops. You can very easily integrate math activities in the study of distance from one address or location to another. Discuss how the latest technology can assist us in our travels. Why must this method of travel assistance require accurate addresses?

Refer to Appendix B to record your own curriculum standards.

Other Teacher-Suggested Activities

Activity Thirty-Eight

———◯———

Birthdays

Everyone has a birthday, but there is great variation in our birth dates and months. Continue reviewing some of the Days of the Week and Months of the Year (Activities One and Two) suggestions. You may be able to generate activities from those areas that are applicable to birthdays. The following activities will enable students to see the differences in birthdays, while respecting each.

Outlined Suggested Activities

1. Start off with a lively discussion about birthdays. You may already have a birthday celebration activity for students on their birth dates. It may be a simple "Happy Birthday to You" song. A student might sit in a special place in the classroom or wear a birthday hat on his or her birthday. Whatever the celebration is, enhance it with a variety of activities that can easily be integrated into the curriculum.
2. Have students assist in designing and making a twelve-month calendar. Make sure dates and days of the week are placed accurately on the calendar. Make the calendars attractive, with each month in a different color. Have students write their names on the day and month on which they were born. Some students may need assistance. Include your birthday on the calendar. Students are now able to see the diversity of their classmates' birth dates. They might see several situations such as:

- Same dates
- Same months
- Most popular months for birthdays for their class

3. Always do something special in your classroom for every child on his or her birthday. Know what is acceptable for each of your students, making sure you are familiar with their culture. Develop a process by which you can also do the same for students who may not be in school on their birthday or have a birthday during the summer months. If snacks are brought in on birthdays, make sure you adhere to school and board policies and guidelines. If food is not allowed, there may be other celebratory activities that can be done.
4. Mathematics: List students on their birthday by their birth month. Develop mathematical problems based on percentages and fractions. (Example: out of the total number of students in the class, what is the percentage of students with birth dates in the top three months?) Continue developing all types of math problems for students to solve. What is the top birthday month?
5. Have students research famous people who share their birthday. Continue researching famous people. You may want to select categories that interest students such as singers, scientists, teachers, astronauts, and/or world leaders.
6. Music: Create a class birthday song with your students. This will give all students an opportunity to have input in a tradition used in class for all students on their birthday.
7. History: Have students research whether a specific historical event occurred on their birthdays (example: launching of a space shuttle).

Refer to Appendix B to record your own curriculum standards.

Other Teacher-Suggested Activities

Activity Thirty-Nine

Numbers

CONSIDER AN EXPLORATION OF numbers as a theme to express and teach diversity. Whether we are young or old, our daily lives are driven by some form of numbers, which is another way to examine the need for diversity. Have students share where they see numbers when they first start off their day. The following suggestions should open the door to other curricular-related activities to enhance a study of diversity and our dependence on different numbers.

OUTLINED SUGGESTED ACTIVITIES

1. Begin a conversation about the significance of numbers in our lives by discussing how numbers impact today's activities. Take an historical tour and explore the power of numbers for people long ago. Below are only several of many ideas relating to numbers:

    - What time did you get up this morning?
    - What time did you leave for school? Were the numbers (time) the same?
    - What time does school start?
    - How many times did the bell ring today?
    - How much was the cost of your pencil?
    - What is the salary of a doctor?

    Students will be able to share even more on numbers and begin to realize how much we depend on them. They help us to understand what, how, and when to do things. Numbers allow us to maintain a certain amount of order in our

daily lives. All the questions above focus on numbers. They are significant to our success and our existence. Continue to expand your list so that students will get a clear understanding of living with numbers all around us.
2. Assign students the task of gathering information on the different uses of numbers over a period of several days. Have them compile their own list on how we live by numbers. Remind them each day to gather information from newspapers, magazines, the Internet, visiting stores with their parents, listening to the weather report, and multiple other sources. They should document their resources in a "Numbers Journal." Prepare some type of documentation form for students to use to collect number data.
3. Social Studies and History: Talk with students about the importance of numbers as you discuss and study history and various historical dates. Discuss how we use numbers to establish a "time" in history. Examples include the significance of 1776, 1820, 2009, and any year of your choosing as it relates to history.
4. Group students to research the use and importance of numbers relating to, but not limited to:

- Telling time
- Buying merchandise/groceries
- Paying bills
- Counting money
- Temperature
- Weight and height
- Health matters (blood pressure, heart rates, cholesterol levels, caloric intake, weight, etc.)
- Age, addresses, and telephone numbers

Develop several fun activities around the above and other categories to show how diverse the use of numbers can be and the need for that diversity.

5. Mathematics: Utilize math internet sites for numerous games, lessons, and activities you can use with your students that emphasize numbers and the importance of numbers in our lives.
6. Mathematics: Develop mathematics lessons around a comparison of various types of numbers and their importance. A few examples are:

- Fractions
- Decimals
- Whole numbers
- Even numbers
- Integers
- Negatives and positives
- Greater and lesser

Why do we need this diversity and variation? Continue developing various fun activities. Using this theme can be very beneficial in teaching students who may not enjoy math. With planning and creativity, you can engage students in multiple activities in which they are learning, having fun, and gaining a better understanding of the world.

Refer to Appendix B to record your own curriculum standards.

Other Teacher-Suggested Activities

Activity Forty

Punctuation

WELCOME TO AN EXCITING THEME! How much do we depend on the use of punctuation marks as we speak and write? A sentence cannot live without these! The proper use of punctuation does not take place only in a language arts class; as adults and children, we use these marks throughout life, and their proper use can make life so much easier.

You may have already worked with the four basic sentence types theme (Activity Thirty-Two). Let us now examine the basic punctuation marks. Punctuation marks are all around us, but quite often we are not conscious of them, or their variety and importance. Envision communicating and writing without the use of punctuation marks. The following activities for this theme will get you started on the study of punctuation marks. Create and enjoy!

OUTLINED SUGGESTED ACTIVITIES

1. Language Arts: Introduce students to a study of four or five basic punctuation marks. If you would like to venture further with more punctuation marks, feel free to do so. But in this resource guide, we will address the major punctuation marks.
2. The major punctuation marks are the period, exclamation mark, question mark, and comma. A number of sources discuss and explain fourteen to fifteen different punctuation marks. Start small and progress. Explain your study as you feel appropriate, first with discussion and then classroom activities. Research the best approaches to use with your students.

3. Reading: Have your class select a children's story or book to read together, such as "The Three Little Pigs" or *Charlotte's Web*. Discuss the punctuation in the story. How do punctuation marks give meaning to sentences and to an entire story? Work with activities on removing punctuation marks. Give examples to students to study and discuss.
4. Assign a group of sentences that require different punctuation marks to groups of students to discuss, and have the groups properly place the punctuation marks. When students have completed this task as a group or team, have them share on the blackboard or Smart Board.
5. Technology: Conduct punctuation and sentence activities using the Smart Board. Look at teacher resources on the Internet that allow students to do independent work on punctuation marks. Utilize various educational websites for fun hands-on activities.
6. Have students bring in short news articles to share with the class and have them explain why certain punctuation marks are used in sentences. This will require students to understand the different functions of the punctuation marks. This can also become a great in-class activity. Bring lots of newspapers to class. Allow students to cut out various short articles and share these.
7. Work with your entire class as they design a "Jeopardy Punctuation" game. Develop sentences and assign the appropriate punctuation. The student responding first with the correct punctuation receives points. Continue to revise and enhance the game.
8. Art: Use the punctuation theme to develop a short skit or play. All students can become actively involved in developing the play. If possible, ask parents to help design costumes and present a mini-play for an open house, Curriculum Night, or PTA gathering. Be creative. Have students develop the narrative with your assistance and portray the punctuation characters.
9. Music: Have students create a punctuation song or rap. The lyrics should indicate the purpose and function of each punctuation mark. This will test whether or not students comprehend the purpose and meaning of each of the punctuation marks. This activity is educational and also lots of fun.
10. Work to design activities to teach punctuation around the eight multiple intelligences.
11. Create short writing assignments in which students are responsible for inserting the correct punctuation mark. Make the writing activities exciting by using themes of interest to your students, such as the top five pop songs, newest technology or social media, latest clothing and hair styles, or favorite foods. As students engage in punctuation activities, they will begin to comprehend the importance of each type of punctuation mark, its uniqueness and diversity, and how each adds to a better understanding of text and improved writing skills.
12. Poetry: Work with students on creating poems that tell us about the basic punctuation marks.

Refer to Appendix B to record your own curriculum standards.

Other Teacher-Suggested Activities

Activity Forty-One

Sports Mascots

INTEGRATING SPORTS INTO THE study of diversity will certainly create lots of energetic sharing of ideas and pride, and even some debate. Tailor your discussion so that all students can engage in these rich activities. Introduce information about local sports teams. Start first with the mascot of your school, and study mascots from other schools, colleges, universities, and professional sports teams. Try to share information students may not know about mascots. Why do certain mascots represent certain schools? Is there a specific history behind the mascot?

OUTLINED SUGGESTED ACTIVITIES

1. Develop activities around the theme of mascots. The local newspaper is an excellent resource for students. This should also motivate students to engage in reading the newspaper. Start off with students reading about various baseball, basketball, soccer, and football teams. You may decide to select other sports. Sometimes girls do not get excited about particular sports. Make sure you integrate a wide range of sports that may be of interest to both males and females.
2. Continue to explore other sports and mascots through reading newspapers and studying national and international online news. This will give different perspectives and viewpoints, and show how diverse the reporting of information can be. Explore and discuss mascots that may not be well known to your students.
3. These hands-on activities are great for moving students into writing and mathematics assignments. Have students talk about their favorite mascots and why they are favorites. Have them explore the following items about mascots:

- The type of sport the mascot represents
- Why the mascot was selected
- Team colors
- School, college, or professional team represented
- Team location (city, state, or country)

Ask students to research their mascot and team by cutting out articles and pictures from newspapers and searching on the Internet. Collect a series of articles and pictures. Put them together in a team collage. Each student can develop a personal collage. The collage should be assembled so that it tells a story about the team.

4. Mathematics: Students can find figures on winning seasons, scores per game, number of games played, and so on. They can compare statistics for various teams. Using the players' jersey numbers, students can work on math problems that you create.
5. Student teams can share reports on various teams with mascots. Develop a standard format so that all students report on factors such as:

- Name of the team and history behind it
- Team colors, mascot, and school represented
- Other information you deem to be appropriate

All of this is specific information. It is a good idea for all students to hear about each team. They will learn from this experience and will have an opportunity to appreciate the diversity each team has to offer.

6. Start a "Mascot Day" at your school. Each student can wear his or her team colors and jerseys.
7. Invite athletes or coaches in the community to your class and talk about their team, mascot, colors, and facts about their school or college. Also ask them to talk about the respect they exhibit for their opponents.
8. Language Arts: Create with your students a team mascot radio show. Have students write scripts with facts about their teams and serve as radio announcers. Create a puppet show about mascots. Continue to be creative in your activities on mascots. This has a potential to show so much diversity among sports teams.
9. Technology: Create a PowerPoint presentation on facts about team mascots that many of your students may not know. This will provide a means of comparison and will help students gain a greater appreciation and respect for other teams and their mascots.

Refer to Appendix B to record your own curriculum standards.

Other Teacher-Suggested Activities

Activity Forty-Two

Newspapers

THE SUGGESTED ACTIVITIES ARE designed to showcase different sections of a newspaper's wide range of information, and newspapers as a means of acquiring knowledge about local, state, and national issues. You will find that some students prefer one section of the newspaper, while others prefer another. We as adults also have preferences. The following activities can be used for independent study, groups, teams, and whole-class lessons on different themes. Use the newspaper as an additional fun resource. Compare and contrast the similarities and differences among various newspapers.

OUTLINED SUGGESTED ACTIVITIES

1. Bring enough newspapers to class for your initial activities. Often companies will donate multiple copies to schools. Try to provide each student his or her own copy so that the shared information will be identical. Some students may not at first find newspapers to be interesting, but use this valuable and universal medium to study. Allow students to read through their copy of the newspaper.
2. So much of a newspaper's diversity can be discovered on the front page. Talk about how it opens the door to what is contained within the rest of the paper. Discuss and illustrate the makeup of the front page with an overhead projector or your Smart Board. There are multiple activities you can design around the front page alone.
3. Mathematics: What is the date on the paper? On what date was the paper established? For how many years has the paper been in circulation? Develop

other math problems using the newspaper. The sales section of the paper can provide a wide range of math problems. Identify the primary news categories one might find in the newspaper, such as:

- Front page
- Sports
- State
- Local
- National
- World
- Opinion, features, classified, etc.

4. Assign pages of interest to your students. Use their multiple intelligence preferences in your assignment. For example, some students may enjoy the arts. If so, assign them pages to read relating to arts, music, drama, and/or entertainment. Get your students involved in newspaper activities several times during the week.
5. Students should become comfortable with their pages of interest. Move to other pages. Design ways to motivate students to get involved in pages where they may have little interest. Continue moving through the entire newspaper.
6. Social Studies: Conduct a weekly study of countries examined in the newspaper. Locate these countries on the map or globe. Get involved in a study of the economy and education of these countries. Integrate other areas of interest in your class study of countries.
7. Language Arts: Use articles from the newspaper to continue your study of the different types of sentences and punctuation marks. Conduct a word study. Rewrite articles.
8. Technology: Designate students to pull out different articles written on technology. Cut out different articles and assign students the responsibility of classifying articles.
9. Field Trips: Take your class on a field trip to the local newspaper office and tour the office to find out more about the impact of newspapers on our lives.
10. Assign students to portray different types of news reporters, such as meteorologists. Have several students research, prepare, and present a weather report for your local area. Make sure they use the appropriate language for the specific category, such as barometric pressure, cloud cover, temperature, highs, and lows.
11. Bring to class newspapers that are written in different languages. Research and discuss. If you can team with another teacher who speaks another language, have that teacher help discuss and explain the news. If you have students from different cultures who would like to bring in a newspaper written in their native language, do this too. Invite parents who represent different cultures to come to your class to discuss their own newspaper.

Refer to Appendix B to record your own curriculum standards.

Other Teacher-Suggested Activities

Activity Forty-Three

Musical Instruments

CREATE A "MOVERS AND SHAKERS" classroom by using the theme of musical instruments to shed light on the need for and advantages of diversity. The suggested activities will help students comprehend the importance of diversity. If you play an instrument, use this theme to create music in your classroom. These activities will certainly help students with various learning styles and multiple intelligences. Work with students as they study instruments being invented and played.

Study the history of gourd musical instruments and help students find out more about gourds and how they are used to produce musical sounds. Examples of various unique and unusual instruments in your classroom would add to your study of diversity, meaning, and sound. You will be able to engage all students in this learning experience.

OUTLINED SUGGESTED ACTIVITIES

Get students involved and excited by having them identify their favorite musical instrument. Once every student has established his or her favorite instrument, talk about the instruments students have in common. Have students identify songs played by or featuring their instrument.

1. Pair students who have an interest in the same instrument. Assign them a task such as researching the history and country of origin of the instrument; famous musicians who play it; songs that feature the instrument; primary musical environments such as orchestra, band, stand-alone, and so on; classification of the instrument (string, percussion, etc.); and inventor of the instrument.

2. Music: Play DVDs of various instruments and work with students as they identify the instruments from the sound. Utilize the Internet for this activity.
3. Invite guests or parents who play an instrument to visit your classroom, share its history, and play for the class.
4. Select a variety of music for certain times in the school day, and play these for the students. Have students identify the instrument in the selections. Try to select pieces that showcase different instruments. Talk about the different sounds instruments make.
5. If you have students who play instruments such as the drums, guitar, violin, trumpet, or piano, have them play for the class.
6. Share with students instruments they are not familiar with, and talk about the history and country of origin.
7. Research famous musicians. Give details on the musician as well as the musical instrument. What type of musical background must one have to play specific instruments?
8. Art: As a part of the historical research on musical instruments, have students draw or make replicas of ancient musical instruments. They may also have an opportunity to make and compare these with similar instruments of today, such as comparing ancient and modern drums.
9. Technology: Develop a PowerPoint presentation about the major classes of instruments, with examples of wind, string, percussion, electronic, and keyboard instruments. This will inform students about the diversity within each category, by sharing the many different types of string instruments, and so on.
10. History and Social Studies: Work with students on a study of ancient musical instruments and the purposes of each. The following are some instruments you might consider researching: flute, rattle, drum, clapper, zither, and bells. There are many more that you might decide to address in your classroom.
11. Technology: Research and discuss the changes to the music world as a result of modern-day technology. Have various high-tech approaches changed many of our musical instruments?

Refer to Appendix B to record your own curriculum standards.

Other Teacher-Suggested Activities

Activity Forty-Four

Colleges and Universities

THESE ACTIVITIES ARE DESIGNED TO introduce the diversity of colleges and universities, but will also spark interest in colleges/universities that students may want to attend someday. Ask other personnel at your school to help carry out various classroom and school activities. Call on your school counselor to work collaboratively with you on this theme. Your students may be at the early elementary level, but these activities can be geared for kindergarten through the eighth grade. The hope is that these activities will help to increase student interest in students to attend an institution of higher education.

Quite often students are familiar with colleges and universities in their immediate area. They may have knowledge of some others, but these activities will introduce them to myriad institutions of higher learning that may spark an interest. Help students expand their knowledge.

OUTLINED SUGGESTED ACTIVITIES

1. Start off with a discussion in your class about colleges and universities in the United States. Invite students to name their college/university of choice. There may be some overlap in favorite institutions. With this list, students will be able to see the range of diversity as it relates to college size, outstanding academic programs, athletic programs, types and levels of degrees offered, and location within or outside your state.
2. Make a chart of the colleges represented, and place the chart in the classroom where it is easily visible to all students. Remind students of the need to fully prepare themselves to attend their institution of choice.

3. Invite your school counselor to talk with the class and perhaps give a PowerPoint presentation on several colleges/universities and their special features. Invite people who have attended different colleges/universities to speak with your students. Talk about how to prepare to attend college.
4. Art: Have students design attractive college/university banners to display in the classroom. Make them large and colorful, representing the schools' colors. List the names of students on the banner of the school they would like to attend. Some may have several choices, and that is okay. After banners have been completed and displayed, develop activities where students engage in in-depth studies of the colleges and universities posted.
5. Research: Set guidelines as to what will be included in the classroom college/university reports. Include such things as school mascot, school colors, location, outstanding programs and areas of study, famous people who attended the institution, family members of students who attended the institution, and so forth.
6. Field Trip: You may have a local college or university in your area. Network with your school and college contacts to invite your class on campus for a tour. Your goal throughout this theme of study is to make available information on several colleges and universities, allowing students to compare and contrast. You may wish to expand your study to international colleges/universities. Encourage students to ask:

    - What colleges/universities are of interest to me?
    - What sets this college/university apart from others?
    - What other important facts do I know about a particular college/university?
    - What are the admission requirements?

7. Exploration: Take several weeks to study, share, and discuss colleges and universities. Select eight to ten, depending on the age level of your students. Give your class the opportunity to discuss, vote on, and reach a consensus about the selected institutions. Encourage a selection of higher institutions throughout the United States. By doing so, your class will end up with a wide geographic representation.
8. Social Studies and Mathematics: Develop "facts" centered on these colleges/universities and prepare a "Know Your Favorite College/University" game for your students. You can also develop flash cards. Have students help prepare these.
9. Make a chart of the interests expressed by your students based on their career choices. Research and share information on colleges/universities that do well in preparing students for these career choices. Have each student research the programs and compare the similarities and differences in the programs/careers of choice. For example, a student may be interested in a specific college's school of dentistry; you can share information on several other colleges with strong dental programs.

10. Language Arts: Finalize the study of this theme by having students pre-write, edit, write, revise, finalize, and present a one-page essay on a college/university of their choice. Invite your school counselor and principal as special guests to listen to student presentations. This activity will assist students in getting up in front of a group and sharing a persuasive piece of writing that expresses their personal views. After students have read their essays, have the counselor and principal make a few brief comments encouraging students to work hard to pursue their dreams.
11. Remember to use the expertise of your school/community professionals to assist with this theme. School counselors will be able to provide more insight on how this theme can be approached and enhanced.

Refer to Appendix B to record your own curriculum standards.

Other Teacher-Suggested Activities

Activity Forty-Five

Parts of a Tree

SCIENCE IS A NATURAL WAY TO GET students involved in diversity. There are numerous themes you can incorporate, with an emphasis on diversity and its benefits. Start by using themes that all students can relate to and participate in through discussions, special projects, and hands-on activities. Science is an excellent subject in which to incorporate themes that incorporate various learning styles and multiple intelligences. Please review your science grade level standards as you embark on these exciting activities.

OUTLINED SUGGESTED ACTIVITIES

1. Science: Take a nature walk and discuss the various types of trees with your students. This will get them comfortable with the theme before they begin documenting their findings. Make sure you first conduct a study of different types of trees in your immediate area.
2. Have your students complete drawings of what they observe. Have them write about the colors of the tree, leaf descriptions, size of the tree, and so on. Before your outside excursion, conduct a thorough study of trees so that students will know what they will observe and draw. Also, have students document the environment in which the trees are located. Provide a format for students to use to document their scientific findings. Sketch out your area beforehand so students will be studying different trees. This will provide more diversity when students share findings.

3. Mathematics: Have students measure or estimate and record findings: circumference, length, leaf measurements, and distance from other objects in inches, feet, and yards.
4. Art: Students should present their findings with several drawings of their tree(s) from several different positions. The differences in how the trees appear shed light on diversity from different perspectives.
5. Technology: Work with students as they access the Internet to find information about the different types of trees. How do these compare with the types of trees in your immediate community?
6. Music: Create a tree song or rap with your entire class, or separate your class into two or three groups. As a part of the song/rap, make sure each group includes a scientific description of a particular tree type, possible uses for that type of tree, and the functions of its parts. The song/rap must be scientifically correct. This is fun learning, yet educational. Students can even engage in a song or rap competition! Discuss the diversity presented.
7. Science: Conduct with your students a detailed project on eight different parts of a tree: crown, trunk, heartwood bark, phloem, cambium, xylem, and root. Divide students into groups, with each group studying a specific part and its purpose. Again, use websites to present in class to make the study come alive with your students.
8. Art: Construct a large tree in the classroom, with each major part labeled. You may also be able to construct and display the project in a special location in your school for others to see and experience. Underneath each of the labels for the parts of the tree, write on card strips the function and purpose of each.
9. Language Arts: Discuss the importance of each tree part and its function to the existence and survival of the entire tree. Have students write short essays on each, and share in the classroom. Help students connect how each separate part contributes to the whole. Ask students questions such as, "What if we did not have the cambium of the tree, and how would this impact the tree itself?"
10. Talk about what might happen to the tree if a part is missing, not functioning properly, or diseased. Compare to the parts of the human body. This will lead to a better understanding of the diversity of functions, and the need for each part to keep the tree healthy, strong, and growing.
11. Social Studies: How does society depend on trees? A number of activities can be developed around this question.
12. Environmental Studies: Invite a horticulturalist to accompany students on a short nature field trip to discuss how trees impact the environment, and the need to protect and grow trees. Plant and care for several trees on your campus. Discuss how trees both positively and negatively impact animal life in the immediate environment.

Refer to Appendix B to record your own curriculum standards.

OTHER TEACHER-SUGGESTED ACTIVITIES

Activity Forty-Six

Jobs and Occupations

STUDENTS ARE ALREADY PREPARING THEMSELVES for their future careers. Some may feel that preparation will start in high school or college. This is not the case. Students in kindergarten, first, and second grades are laying the foundation for what they will do with their lives. It is important to share this message and integrate these thoughts and discussions into all areas of study.

Numerous fun and exciting activities can focus on the theme of jobs, which will affect every student in your classroom. You have had the opportunity to learn about each student, his or her strengths, learning style, and multiple intelligence preferences. You should have a general idea of what career each student may want to pursue.

OUTLINED SUGGESTED ACTIVITIES

1. Newspaper activities: Use the newspapers to get students reading and excited about discussing the many different occupations and jobs available. Have your students select several news articles and identify the occupation(s) associated with the articles. They should read the articles in order to assign a profession or occupation to a particular article.
2. Select several children's books that depict different occupations and read these to your students. Discuss preparation needed for these occupations.
3. Have all students talk about what job they want as adults. Make a giant list of these occupations and post in the classroom. Classify the occupations into categories, such as law, business and finance, education, food

distribution, athletics/sports, and so on. Talk about the diversity of these categories. Center the discussion of the occupations around "why selected" and "preparation needed." Students will be able to focus on the diversity of occupations and jobs.

4. Technology: Have students explore websites on various categories of occupations, such as science, religion, special education, law, and medicine.
5. Invite a panel of guests to come in and talk about their careers. Take a field trip so students can see various people at work and discover what they do as a part of their job.
6. Invite your school counselor to come in several times and talk with students about career preparation.
7. With your students, develop a list of famous people and research their careers and the preparations they have made. Select people from a number of areas of expertise who would serve as positive role models for students as they engage in individual research.
8. Work with students on a "Parade of Occupations" that involves wearing a piece of clothing that represents a particular profession, and perhaps bringing in an associated prop, such as a stethoscope for the medical profession. Each student must share several facts about the profession. Invite parents to attend the parade.
9. Language Arts: Select one occupation each week, and ask students to work on a creative writing response to the questions: "What would the world be like without this occupation?" and "How would the lack of this profession impact all of us?"
10. Critical Thinking: Get involved in a critical thinking discussion with students by asking students: "If every person had the same job, such as doctor, or a farmer, pilot, or teacher, what type of world would we have?" Listen to the students as they share and discuss. Continue to discuss and share the need for diversity when it comes to occupations and jobs.

Refer to Appendix B to record your own curriculum standards.

Other Teacher-Suggested Activities

Summary

It has been a joy and a privilege to prepare this resource guide for you, the reader. Reading, preparing, and researching have truly taken me on an extraordinary educational journey that I will never forget. One of the greatest personal rewards has been talking with teachers about diversity, and finding out what would help them teach while creating a deeper appreciation for diversity. Speaking with educators throughout the United States has encouraged me to continue to research and write resources that will benefit teachers through user-friendly and cost-effective approaches.

We do not have to search for "diversity." We look around and it is there. Teachers often express that discussing race, gender, religion, and cultural diversity is sometimes uncomfortable. One goal of this guide is to share diversity themes that teachers can use to introduce students to various dimensions of diversity.

Once this has been accomplished, dimensions of diversity that tend to be sensitive topics can now be shared and discussed more openly and comfortably. If we strive to become the best and most effective teachers we can be, we *must* include diversity awareness exploration and conversation as one of our instructional approaches.

You now have in your hands forty-six themes accompanied with a multiplicity of energizing academic activities. There is no limit to the themes to be explored. Go for it! Develop other themes of your choice. This will be an opportunity for all teachers to address and discuss race, gender, religion, and other sensitive dimensions of diversity more openly. In doing so, maybe, just maybe we can educate and prepare young people for the world they will be a part of and will shape for many generations to come.

Appendix A
Lesson-Plan Format: Diversity Awareness

Standard Stated: (CCSS; ES; SS; Other) _____

_____

_____

Content: _____ Grade Level _____

Activity Type: ☐ Whole Class ☐ Group ☐ Individual

Theme: _____ Date: _____

Introduction to this theme: _____

_____

_____

Notes on instructional practices addressing learners: _____

_____

_____

Teacher-directed activities: _____

_____

_____

Student-directed practices: _____
_____
_____

Comments on outcome of lesson: _____
_____
_____

Possible lesson plan modification: _____
_____
_____

Overall assessment of student success:

☐ Fair   ☐ Good   ☐ Very Good   ☐ Excellent   ☐ Other

Level of student involvement: ☐ Low   ☐ Medium   ☐ High

Comments: _____
_____
_____

Research findings: _____
_____

Appendix B
Curriculum Standards

CURRICULUM STANDARDS IDENTIFICATION/INFORMATION

GRADE: _____ CONTENT: _____

Common Core State Standard Number: _____

Common Core State Standard Stated: _____

_____

Essential Standard Number: _____

Essential Standard Stated: _____

_____

State Standard Number: _____

State Standard Stated: _____

_____

Outcome Information: _____

_____

_____

Reflections:

_____

_____

_____

_____

Appendix C
Teacher-Suggested Themes

LIST POSSIBLE THEMES THAT IDENTIFY dimensions of diversity and provide academic lessons instrumental for student achievement. Develop activities around your selected themes.

- _____
- _____
- _____
- _____
- _____
- _____
- _____
- _____
- _____
- _____

Appendix C

- _____
- _____
- _____
- _____
- _____
- _____
- _____
- _____
- _____
- _____
- _____
- _____
- _____
- _____
- _____
- _____
- _____
- _____
- _____
- _____

Bibliography

BOOKS AND ARTICLES

Cushner, K., P. McClelland, and P. Safford. *Human Diversity in Education: An Intercultural Approach*. 8th ed. Boston: McGraw-Hill, 2014.

Echevarria, Jana, and Ann Graves. *Sheltered Content Instruction*. 4th ed. Boston: Pearson Education, 2011.

Ginsberg, Margery. "Culturally Diverse Classrooms." *Educational Leadership* 72, no. 6 (March 2015). http://www.ascd.org/publications/educational-leadership/mar15/vol72/num06/Making-Diverse-Classrooms-Safer-for-Learning.aspx.

Gust, J., J. McChesney, and M. Burr. *Appreciating Differences: Multicultural Thematic Units*. Carthage, IL: Teaching and Learning Company, 1995. (Grades 3–6).

Heacox, Diane. *Differentiating Instruction in the Regular Classroom: How to Reach and Teach All Learners, Grades 3–12*. Minneapolis: Free Spirit, 2002.

Hill-Jackson, V., K. Sewell, and C. Waters. "Having Our Say About Multicultural Education." *Kappa Delta Pi Record* 43, no. 4 (Summer 2007): 149–92.

Jansen, Jonathan, J. Lynn McBrien, Jean Moule, and Yong Zhao. "The Color of Learning: Embracing Diversity." *Phi Delta Kappan* 90, no. 5 (January 2009): 313–92.

Koppelman, Kent, and R. Lee Goodhart. *Human Differences: Multicultural Education for a Diverse America*. 3rd ed. Boston: Pearson Education, 2011.

Lamia, Mary C. *Understanding Myself: A Kid's Guide to Intense Emotions and Strong Feelings*. Washington, DC: Magination Press, November 2010.

Levin, Ina, S. Fullam, and K. Vascancelles. *Celebrating Diversity*. Huntington Beach, CA: Teacher Created Materials, 1993.

Lipson, Greta, and Bernice N. Greenberg. *Extra! Extra! Read All About It!* Carthage, IL: Good Apple, 1981.

Miller, Susan, F. "Teachers as Co-Learners and Advocates for Diversity." *Thinking Classroom* 4, no. 3 (International Reading Association) (2003): 21–28.

Moran, S., M. Kornhaber, and H. Gardner. "Orchestrating Multiple Intelligences." *Educational Leadership* 64, no. 1 (September 2006): 22–27.

North Carolina Professional Teaching Standards Commission. *North Carolina Teaching Standards.* Raleigh: North Carolina Department of Public Instruction, 2006.

Oakes, Jennie, and Marvin Lipton. *Teaching to Change the World.* 3rd ed. Boston: McGraw-Hill, 2006.

Paraskevas, B., and M. Paraskevas. *The Kids from Room 402 (Grace Graves and the Kids from Room 402).* Hong Kong: Simon & Schuster Children's Publishing, 2000. (Ages 4–8)

Schwartz, D., Jessica Tsang, and Kristen Blair. *The ABC's of How We Learn: 26 Scientifically Proven Approaches, How They Work, and When to Use Them.* New York: W. W. Norton and Company, 2016.

Other Resources

Education Week: American Education's Newspaper of Record. www.edweek.org.

International Literacy Association. www.literacyworldwide.org.

Interstate New Teachers Assessment and Support Consortium (InTASC). http://www.ccsso.org/Resources/Programs/Interstate_Teacher_Assessment_Consortium_(InTASC).html.

Teaching Tolerance: A Project of the Southern Poverty Law Center. www.tolerance.org.

Willis, Judy. *Cognitive Priming Students for Learning.* Edutopia, 2014. https://www.edutopia.org/blog/cognitively-priming-students-for-learning-judy-willis.

About the Author

Rona Leach McLeod has been in education for over forty years, serving as a classroom teacher, school administrator, central office administrator, and associate professor of education at St. Andrews University, a branch of Webber International University. She writes children's books and resource materials for teachers.

McLeod holds a Bachelor of Arts degree and two Master degrees. She received her doctorate in educational leadership from Nova University, now known as Nova Southeastern University, in Ft. Lauderdale, Florida. She believes teachers are truly "action researchers," constantly addressing problems, working to find solutions to problems, and seeking more effective ways of teaching and preparing young people for their future.

McLeod enjoys reading, researching, writing, and teaching. Cooking with her husband, Herbert, brings her great joy. She resides in Marston, North Carolina, with her husband and their dog, Zorro.